A 90 Day Journey with God

*Daily spiritual reflections
to light the way in a changing world*

A 90 DAY JOURNEY WITH GOD

Daily spiritual reflections to light the way in a changing world

Copyright © 2025 Ronald Hale

Scripture References

Unless otherwise noted, all Scripture quotations are taken from multiple translations of the Bible, including but not limited to the New International Version (NIV), New Living Translation (NLT), English Standard Version (ESV), New King James Version (NKJV), and The Message (MSG). All rights for these translations are held by their respective copyright holders.

Scripture has been used with reverence and care to honor the integrity and truth of God's Word.

ISBN: 979-8-9880626-8-4
LCCN:

10 9 8 7 6 5 4 3 2 1

Printed in the United States of America
(Paperback) First Edition: August 2025

SITE PUBLISHING
7330 Staples Mill Road #106
Richmond, VA 23228

Author Information
Ronald Hale

Website: https://www.ronhalebooks.com
Email: sitepublishingtoday@gmail.com

All of my blogs can be found at **https://www.ronhalebooks.com/blog** a space where I share honest, faith-filled reflections to encourage your walk with God and speak life into your everyday journey.

Thank You

First and always, to God. Thank You for never giving up on me. I'm humbled that You would choose to use my life and my words to share Your truth with the world. Every blog, every sentence, every moment I wanted to quit, You carried me. May this book bring You glory and draw hearts back to You.

To the greatest mother on the planet. You are the reason I am the man I am today. Your prayers, sacrifices, and love kept me going through every challenge. I am so thankful for you, and I love you more than words can say.

To my Uncle Lee. Thank you for teaching me to stay true to God and to myself. You will be deeply missed, but your legacy lives on in me.

To those who believed in me, spoke life into me, and said, ***"You need to put the blogs in a book,"*** thank you. Your faith in what God was doing through me kept me going more than you know.

To everyone who has read the blogs, shared them, or sent an encouraging message, I'm so grateful. Your support reminded me that the words were making a difference, and that was more than enough.

This book is also for the ones who have felt unseen, overlooked, or invisible. If that's you, please hear this: God has been walking with you the entire way. Even in the silence. Even when you felt all alone. When no one else noticed you, He did. He never looked away. And He never left.

And finally, to my beautiful daughter, Ryan. You are my heartbeat. On the darkest days, you've been my light. Watching you grow, love, and shine has been one of the greatest gifts of my life. You remind me what really matters. This book carries pieces of you on every page.

The Lord answered me: "Write down the vision; write it clearly on clay tablets so whoever reads it can run to tell others."

Habakkuk 2:2 (NCV)

Day 1

Don't Forget the Cane

Oftentimes, I like to start my writings with a quote I recently came across, and this time is no different. But first, let me ask you something: Have you ever heard someone say, **"Don't forget where you came from,"** or **"Don't forget the little people when you make it big"?**

I've heard those words from family, friends, and mentors growing up, but it wasn't until I came across this quote that their meaning really sank in.

"The day the blind man sees is the day he throws away the cane that has helped him his whole life."

That quote really makes you stop and think. It says a lot about people: how we change, how we forget, and how growing in faith means learning to love with wisdom, not just emotion.

Maybe we weren't physically blind, but we've all gone through seasons of spiritual blindness. Blind to truth, blind to love, blind to our God-given purpose. And in those moments, we leaned on something or someone to keep us going: a friend, a belief, a habit, maybe even a crutch. That 'cane' helped us walk when we couldn't stand on our own.

But what happens when our eyes *finally* open? When things start to make sense: our path, our purpose, even the people around us?

What happens to the cane?

In **John 9**, Jesus heals a man blind from birth. When questioned, the man says, ***"One thing I do know: I was blind, but now I see."*** – **John 9:25**

Spiritual sight doesn't just change what we see, **it changes how we see.** We start to realize who was really with us, and who was only around when we needed help. That's not bitterness, it's discernment.

I think back on my life before I fully surrendered to Jesus. When I made poor choices, when I couldn't find a way out, somehow I always made it through. I called it luck. I thought I was just in the right place at the right time. But looking back, I see it clearly now: it was God. His mercy. His grace. His hand.

Maybe you've had a similar moment. A time you thought you were making it on your own, only to realize later, it was God carrying you the whole time.

And yet, how often do we forget God's hand in our lives?

We get healed, we get blessed, and we move on. Like the blind man putting away the can, we lay aside the very One who carried us through. We stop praying like we used to. Stop depending. Stop thanking. Sometimes, we even take the credit. Jesus experienced this too. Ten lepers were healed. Only one returned to say thank you. *"Were not all ten cleansed? Where are the other nine?"* – **Luke 17:17**

God's grace not only saves us but transforms us so we can serve others. But in a world that often values **usefulness** over **relationships**, this quote gives us a warning: Not everyone you help will thank you. And not everyone you walk with will walk with you forever.

And we do the same to God.

In **1 Samuel 8**, the Israelites basically told God, *"Thanks, but we want a king we can actually see."* Even after all He had done: rescuing them, taking care of them, showing up over and over, they still wanted something they felt they could control. They forgot it was God who had been carrying them the whole time.

We do too. When life gets hard, we run to God. But when life gets good, we sometimes walk away. We trust the job, the paycheck, the relationship, the status and forget the **Source** of it all.

"He must increase, but I must decrease." – **John 3:30**. John the Baptist understood it was never about him. Every message he preached, every person he reached, he pointed it all back to God. He never forgot the One who gave him vision in the first place. And we shouldn't either.

Take a moment to look back.

Think about the times you didn't know how you were going to make it, the dark seasons, the silent prayers, the moments you almost gave up. It wasn't your own strength that carried you. It was God. His grace. His mercy. His quiet, steady presence when everything else felt unsure.

Now that your eyes are beginning to open. Now that you're walking a little stronger and seeing a little clearer, don't forget Him. Don't treat Him like a cane you only needed when you were weak. The truth is, we never stop needing God.

So stay near to Him. Rest in His Word. Talk to Him like you did when you were desperate. Trust Him like your life depends on it, because it still does.

Ask the Holy Spirit to guide you with wisdom and love. Let Him shape your steps, soften your heart, and keep you humble. Let your life be a reflection of the grace that carried you through.

You are God's creation. He's still working in you. Keep walking with Him. He's not finished with you yet.

Pray with me

Lord,

Thank You for carrying me when I couldn't walk on my own. Thank You for the grace I didn't see at the time. Help me to always remember what You've done for me. Help me honor the people You used to lift me up. Show me when to help others, and give me wisdom to know when to let go. More than anything, let my life bring You glory. Don't let me ever set You aside, Lord. Grow bigger in me.

**In Jesus' name,
Amen.**

Day 2

The Day You Were Born, and the Day You Found Out Why

I was watching a movie today that I've seen many times before. But this time, something stood out; something I'd never noticed until now. As the opening credits rolled, a quote appeared on the screen. It was from *Mark Twain*. He said:

"The two most important days in your life are the day you are born and the day you find out why."

That hit me hard. Most of us know when we were born. But do we know why?

Yes, your birthday matters. It's when your life began. But discovering why you were born? That's when your life truly changes. That's the moment things start to make sense. That's the day purpose comes alive.

So let me ask you: **Do you know your "why"?**

Living isn't just about waking up, working, eating, and sleeping. It's about **purpose**, knowing why you're here and what you were made to do. Life gets clearer when you know that. It feels more full. You stop just existing and start living.

From God's view, this quote means even more. As **Jeremiah 1:5** says, *"Before I formed you in the womb I knew you. Before you were born I set you apart."* God knew you first! Your life is no accident.

The day you were born was a gift. You didn't just show up by chance. God handcrafted you. Your life started with His breath. You were made with care, on purpose, and with purpose. Not for your glory, but for His. **Ephesians 2:10** reminds us, *"For we are God's masterpiece. He created us anew in Christ Jesus, so we can do the good things He planned for us long ago."* Your life is part of His great plan.

And the day you find out why? That's when you wake up to the truth. That's your spiritual turning point; your calling, your purpose, your "why." Sometimes it comes through prayer. Sometimes through pain. Sometimes through a dream, a moment, or a deep pull in your heart that says, **"There's more to life than this."**

When you find your "why," you stop drifting. You stop comparing. You stop chasing things that don't last. You begin living with focus and peace. You start doing things that matter. You start walking in step with God.

Your life is meant to glorify Him and serve others. **Matthew 22:37–39** teaches us to *"Love the Lord your God with all your heart... and love your neighbor as yourself."* This is the heart of your purpose.

So whatever you do; big or small, do it for His glory. Remember **1 Corinthians 10:31**, *"So whether you eat or drink or whatever you do, do it all for the glory of God."* Every part of your life can honor Him.

That means God knew you before anyone else did. He chose you. He called you.

So if you're still searching for your purpose, start by asking God. Talk to Him. He wants to show you. Look at what you care about, what brings you joy, what you're good at. That's often where your "why" begins. Your past matters too. God can use your story to help someone else.

And don't feel like you have to figure it all out today. Finding your "why" is a journey. It takes time. But every step you take toward God will lead you closer.

Your "why" is tied to your relationship with God. If you don't know God, your purpose will always feel out of reach. It won't matter how many books you read, how many people speak into your life, or how hard you try to figure it out. Without God, the "why" fades.

Stop waiting for people to tell you what God has already planted in you.

When you seek Him, truly seek Him and His righteousness, your "why" will begin to rise from the soil of your soul like something that's been waiting to bloom.

Your relationship with God is the most important relationship you will ever have.

Through Him, purpose becomes clear. Through Him, you live with meaning. **God alone is the reason for your why.**

Don't let another day pass living without direction. The God who formed you is still speaking. Seek Him, and you will find your "why."

Pray with me

Lord,

Thank You for creating me on purpose. I know I'm not here by accident. Help me discover why You made me. Show me my purpose, guide my steps, and use my life to bring You glory. I want to live with meaning. I want to walk in Your will.

In Jesus' name,
Amen.

Day 3

Check the Source

When I was a kid, I remember accidentally breaking a mirror and being told, "That's seven years of bad luck." I thought, **Seriously? Seven years? Just for breaking a mirror?** But because it came from someone I trusted, I believed it. And not just that, I believed all kinds of things. Like if a black cat crossed my path, something bad would happen. Or if someone swept my feet with a broom, I'd never get married. I never questioned it. In my young mind, those voices felt true. But I never asked: **Who said that?**

See, when you trust the wrong voice, you'll end up believing a lie.

For years, every time I saw a black cat, I ran in the house like danger was chasing me. Looking back, I realize I was living under self-imposed curses; all because I never checked the source.

We do this more than we realize. We accept what people tell us without asking God if it's true. We build beliefs off of rumors, traditions, or half-truths. And sometimes, it's not even strangers misleading us: it's people we trust.

But the Bible warns us: ***"Dear friends, do not believe every spirit, but test the spirits to see whether they are from God..."*** **(1 John 4:1)**. Just because something *sounds* spiritual or deep doesn't mean it's from God.

Eve learned that the hard way. The serpent didn't come to her looking evil, he came with a smooth voice and a little twist on God's truth. And that one conversation changed everything.

That's why spiritual discernment is so important. In the book of **Acts 17:11**, Paul praised the Bereans for double-checking his message. They didn't just take his word for it. They searched the Scriptures daily to make sure it was true. That's what we need to do. Don't just follow every voice. Go back and ask God.

Because the wrong voice can lead you down a path that was never meant for you. It can delay your destiny. It can leave you spiritually exhausted, emotionally confused, and far from God's best.

We've seen it over and over. People walking in fear and anxiety because someone spoke something over them that didn't line up with God's Word. Maybe someone said, **"You'll never make it,"** or **"You're just like your father,"** or **"You'll always struggle."** And instead of rejecting the lie, you received it. But here's the truth: *Only God has the final word over your life.*

He's the Author and Finisher of your faith, not people, not culture, not tradition.

Scripture warns us not to fall for "old wives' tales" (**1 Timothy 4:7**), those generational sayings and superstitions that get passed down like family recipes, but are rooted in fear, not truth. Just because something has been said for years doesn't mean it's God's voice.

Let's be real: even people with good intentions can mislead you. Take the story in **1 Kings 13**. God gave a prophet specific instructions: don't eat or drink during the assignment, and don't go back the same way. But another man, also claiming to be a prophet, told him, ***"God told me to tell you it's okay. Come eat with me."*** So he did. And because he obeyed man over God, it cost him his life.

Even fellow believers can give you a word that sounds spiritual but isn't from God. That's why you have to **check the source.** Don't move based on someone's title or tone; go back to God. Pray. Ask Him.

Remember when Jesus was fasting in the wilderness for 40 days? Satan came and said, ***"If you're really the Son of God, turn these stones into bread."*** But Jesus didn't argue. He didn't panic. He simply replied, ***"It is written…"*** (**Matthew 4:4**). That's how we fight deception: with God's Word.

And listen: this isn't about living in fear or never trusting anyone. It's about staying grounded in the truth. **James 1:5** says if you lack wisdom, *ask God*, and He'll give it freely. That means God wants to guide you. He wants you to hear His voice.

"My sheep know My voice," Jesus said in **John 10:27**. *Do you recognize His voice?*

When you know the voice of God, it changes everything. You walk with peace. You stop reacting to every opinion. You stop doubting your path. You stop letting people define your future. Why? Because the Shepherd is leading you.

In this noisy, chaotic world, discernment isn't optional, it's survival. **1 Corinthians 2:10** says *the Spirit searches all things.* That's why you need the Holy Spirit. He's the One who gives you insight, clarity, and direction when everything around you feels loud and confusing.

So, the next time someone speaks over you, stop and ask, **"God, is this from You?"** Test it. Search the Word. Listen for His voice. He will never deceive you. He always leads in truth.

And if the voice you're following today isn't pointing you back to God, it's time to check the source.

Remember:
"Not every voice deserves your trust. The wrong voice can cost you your purpose, or even your life. This message is a wake-up call to tune your ear back to the only voice that leads to truth, freedom, and life: the voice of God."

Pray with me

Father God,

Thank You for being the voice I can trust in a world full of noise and confusion. Help me to hear You clearly and to follow You boldly.

I repent for the times I believed lies spoken over me; whether by others, by culture, or by my own fear.

Teach me to test every word I receive and to compare it with Your truth. Give me wisdom, discernment, and peace.

When I don't know what to do, remind me to pause and ask You. You are faithful to answer.

Thank You for being my Shepherd. I am Your sheep, and I want to know Your voice above every other.

Lead me, guide me, and protect me from deception.

In Jesus' name,
Amen.

Day 4

Put the Glass Down

When was the last time you slowed down and made yourself a **priority**?

I don't mean taking a quick nap or watching a show to distract your mind. I mean really stepping away from the pressure, the schedule, the noise, and giving yourself space to be real. To breathe. To stop pretending you're fine when you're not, and just rest, even if just for a moment.

This world keeps us moving nonstop. We've been taught that busy means we're on the right track. But sometimes, busy doesn't mean blessed; it just means overwhelmed. Overwhelmed by expectations, pressure, anxiety, and the fear that if we stop even for a moment, everything might fall apart.

Let me ask you something real. What have you been holding onto lately?

Because today, I saw a video that really made me think. A teacher stood before his class holding a glass of water. He asked, **"How heavy do you think this is?"** People threw out numbers,

8 ounces, 12, 16. The teacher nodded and said, **"It's not about the weight. It's about how long I hold it. If I hold it for a minute, nothing happens. If I hold it for an hour, my arm will begin to ache. If I hold it all day, my arm goes numb, even paralyzed. The weight of the glass hasn't changed, but the longer I hold onto it, the heavier it becomes."**

The teacher's point with the glass of water really stuck with me: stress, worry, and all that emotional pressure work the same way. The longer you hold onto them, the heavier they feel. So here's the thing; **put the glass down**.

Maybe you've been holding on too long; holding on to pain you can't quite explain, fears you're scared to admit, or burdens that were never yours to carry in the first place.

Maybe you're caught up in a situation you can't control. Or a relationship that just drains you. Maybe you're holding onto unforgiveness toward someone who hurt you. Or maybe you're just tired of pretending to be strong when no one knows how much you're really struggling.

But here's what I want you to remember: God never asked you to carry that burden. In fact, He tells us, *"Cast all your anxiety on Him, because He cares for you"* (**1 Peter 5:7**). Not just some of it. Not only the parts you feel ready to let go of. All of it.

Even Martha, who loved Jesus deeply; got caught up in doing. She wanted to serve, but she got so overwhelmed, she started comparing herself to her sister and got frustrated. And in her stress, she tried to get Jesus to agree with her frustration. But He looked at her and said, *"Martha, Martha, you are worried and upset about many things, but only one thing is necessary"* **(Luke 10:41–42)**. He wasn't criticizing her, He was inviting her back to what mattered most: **Him**.

And then there's Gideon. He was hiding when God called him a mighty warrior. His response? *"My family is the weakest in Manasseh, and I am the least in my father's house."* **(Judges 6:15)** But God wasn't focused on Gideon's fears or limitations. He was focused on His purpose. And even when Gideon doubted, God stayed with him; patient, present, and faithful.

So listen closely: Jesus isn't asking you to have everything figured out. He's asking you to trust Him. To stop pretending you're okay when you're not. To stop carrying what's wearing you down. And to let Him in, right where you are.

Maybe your heart is whispering, **"But I've carried this for so long…"**
And He's whispering back, **"Then let Me carry you."**

"Come to Me, all who are weary and burdened, and I will give you rest." **(Matthew 11:28)**

That promise isn't for people who have it all figured out. It's for the ones who feel like they're drowning silently. The ones who smile on the outside but are breaking inside. The ones who feel like they have to be the strong one, always.

It's for **you**.

And if nobody else has told you today, let me be the one to say it: **You are not alone. You never were.**

"For God so loved the world that He gave His only Son, so that whoever believes in Him will not perish but have eternal life." (John 3:16)

That love doesn't just cover you, it frees you.

So if the glass is getting heavy, don't ignore it. Don't fake it. And don't carry what Jesus already died to take. **Put it down, not because you're giving up, but because you're giving it to Him.**

Pray with me

God,

I've been carrying stuff You never asked me to carry. The stress, the fear, the pressure to hold it all together; it's too much. And honestly, I'm tired. So today, I'm handing it over to You. All of it. I don't want to pretend I'm fine when I'm not. I need Your peace. I need Your strength. Remind me that I don't have to do this on my own. Thank You for being patient with me. Thank You for staying close. I trust You. Help me rest in that. In Jesus' name, Amen.

**In Jesus' name,
Amen.**

Day 5

You Were Never Meant to Fit In

If you've ever smiled in public while falling apart in private, this is for you.

If you've ever held back tears because you didn't think anyone would understand, you're not the only one. Life can hit hard; mentally, emotionally, spiritually, and sometimes it just feels too personal to put into words, let alone share with anyone .

But if there's one thing I know for sure, it's this: **God is still good.**

And He sees you. He hears you. And He cares more than you know.

June is National Men's Mental Health Awareness Month, and while it shines a light on what many men struggle with quietly, the truth is, **it's a conversation that matters for all of us.** Whether you're a man or a woman, we've all had moments where we smiled on the outside but battled silently on the inside.

I saw a video the other day where a group of men were asked a simple question: **"Who do you call when you're at your lowest?"** Almost every man gave the same answer: **"No one."** That stuck with me. I had to pause and ask myself, who do I turn to when I feel like I'm slipping? And if the answer is no one, why is that?

Is it fear of being misunderstood? Or maybe you're tired of feeling like a burden to everyone. Maybe you've told yourself, **"No one would really get it anyway, or who would care?"** But that's not true.

You may be in a moment right now where you're running on empty. You're doing your best to show up for everyone, but inside, something's breaking. I want you to hear me clearly: you're not weak for feeling tired. You're not broken because you need help. And you're not less of a person for admitting that you're struggling.

God cares. He hears the words you're too afraid to say out loud. He sees every battle you're fighting in secret, and He's not turning away from you. He's drawing closer.

In **1 Samuel 1**, Hannah was in deep pain. She longed for a child and couldn't take the quiet anymore. She went to the temple, **poured out her soul, and prayed from a place only God could understand.** Her husband meant well, but he didn't really get it. Eli the priest saw her and assumed she was drunk. **But God didn't misunderstand her.** He heard her cry and gave her a son that she named Samuel, which means **heard by God**. Her pain turned into purpose, and her tears became part of a greater story.

Hannah didn't wait for permission to be honest about what she was going through. She didn't wait for someone else to validate her pain. **She just took it to God. And He met her right where she was,** and He will do the same for you.

You don't have to hold it all in. You don't have to pretend you're doing well when it feels like your whole world is crumbling around you. You don't have to carry the pressure of being strong for everyone else, anymore. God is inviting you to bring it all to Him. And guess what? **You can trust Him**.

The Bible says, *"Cast all your anxiety on Him because He cares for you"* **(1 Peter 5:7)**. Not just some of it. Not just the parts you think are acceptable. **All of it.**

David understood this too. Just look at the Psalms. **He cried out, he questioned, he worshiped, and through it all, God never turned him away.**

Even Jesus, the Son of God, knelt in the Garden of Gethsemane and said, *"My soul is overwhelmed with sorrow…"* **(Matthew 26:38)**. His friends fell asleep while He was in agony, but the Father never left Him.

You don't have to wait until you got it all together. You don't have to clean up your prayers or edit your emotions. **Just be real with God. He's not afraid of your truth. He's already seen the worst and still loves you with the best.**

As you learn to be honest with God, don't forget, there are people around you who are fighting their own silent battles. They may not need someone to fix them. They just need someone who won't judge them. Someone who will listen. **Be that safe place for someone. And remember this: God is that safe place for you, always.**

If you feel unseen, He sees you. If you feel unheard, He's listening. If you feel like you're slipping, He's still holding on.

You are never alone. Just like God told Joshua, He promises to be with you wherever you go. So take heart, be strong and courageous. Don't let fear or discouragement win, because the Lord your God is right there with you, every step, every moment **(Joshua 1:9)**. Lean into that truth. Hold on to it like your life depends on it, because sometimes, it does.

Pray with me

Father,

Thank You for always being near. Thank You for listening when no one else seems to understand. Today, I bring You the parts of me I've kept hidden. The questions, the fear, the exhaustion. I know You're not afraid of my truth. Heal what hurts. Restore what's worn down. And remind me again that I'm never alone. You are my safe place.

In Jesus' name,
Amen.

Day 6

What You're Running From May Be Your Greatest Victory

Have you ever been asked to do something you just didn't want to do? Something that made you wonder, **"Why me? Why not someone else?"**

I remember my senior year of high school when the basketball coach called an emergency team meeting. We were confused, curious; this had never happened before. When he walked in smiling, we knew something was up. And then he told us the track team had a meet but not enough runners. He challenged us, his basketball players to join the track team for the day.

Why? Because the more people who participated, the more points the team could earn. Every runner added value. Even if we didn't win, our participation itself could help lead to victory.

I laughed inside. I was a basketball player, not a runner. Still, somehow, he convinced all of us. And me? He had me running the 300.

Let me tell you, I wanted no part of it. I made every excuse. "That's not my gift." "I've never done that." "Someone else is better." Sound familiar?

But despite my resistance, there I was, standing on the track. I looked around at the other runners stretching, confident. I knew I didn't belong. But when the starter pistol fired, I ran, hard. Not because I was trained, but because I hated losing. And when the race ended, I came in second. Or so I thought.

The coach approached and said, "Actually, you won. The runner ahead of you stepped into your lane. The victory is yours."

It wasn't skill that brought the win. It was **grace**. It was **alignment**. It was **God showing me something greater than the race. He was teaching me about purpose**.

Sometimes, God will call you to something that makes no sense to you. You'll look around and say, "Why me? I'm not the right one." You'll try to hand off the assignment to someone who looks more qualified, more confident, more spiritual. **But God isn't looking for the most talented, He's looking for the most surrendered.**

Jonah tried to run from his assignment. God said, "Go to Nineveh." Jonah said, "I'd rather not," and went the opposite way. But God didn't change His mind. He redirected Jonah. Even when Jonah sat in the belly of a fish, God still preserved him and brought him back to the mission. Why? Because **God's purposes don't depend on our comfort, they depend on our surrender.**

Moses said, *"I can't speak well."* But God replied, *"Now go; I will help you speak and will teach you what to say"* (**Exodus 4:12**).

Jeremiah said, *"I'm too young,"* and God said, *"Do not say 'I am too young.' You must go to everyone I send you to"* (**Jeremiah 1:7**).

Gideon said, *"I'm the least of my tribe,"* but God called him *"mighty warrior"* and used him to defeat an entire army with just 300 men (**Judges 6**).

You see, the very thing you're running from may be the very thing that brings God the most glory. It's not about whether you feel qualified, it's about **who** is calling you. **And when God calls you, He equips you. He goes with you. He works through you.**

Stop measuring your worth by your ability. Start measuring it by your availability to God.

The track meet wasn't about how fast I could run. It was about showing up, doing what I could, and trusting the outcome. The coach saw something in me I didn't see in myself. **How much more does God see in you?**

There are people, places, and divine moments **assigned to your obedience.** You may not understand how it will all work out, but God does. And **He's not asking you to figure it all out. He's asking you to trust Him.**

Don't be like Jonah, trying to escape the call. Because here's the truth: you can't outrun God. He's everywhere. He knows everything. And He's already prepared the victory. He's just waiting on your yes.

You are not a mistake. You are not overlooked. You are chosen. You are assigned. And you are needed. Every step you take in obedience earns points for the Kingdom of God. Not because you're striving, but because God receives glory when you walk in your purpose.

So... what are you running from? Or better yet, **what are you running toward?**

*"To Him who is able to do immeasurably more than all we ask or imagine, according to His power that is at work within us, to Him be glory in the church and in Christ Jesus throughout all generations, forever and ever! Amen." - **Ephesians 3:20–21***

Pray with me

Father, in the name of Jesus, we thank You for being patient with us, even when we've tried to run. Thank You for being a God who pursues us, redeems us, and still calls us by name. Forgive us for every excuse, every delay, every moment we've doubted Your assignment. Today, we surrender. We give You our yes. Not because we're strong, but because You are. Fill us with courage. Remind us that obedience to You brings glory to Your name and purpose to our lives. Use us, Lord. And let Your will be done.

In Jesus' mighty name. Amen.

Day 7

Take Back the Brush:
Let God Paint Your Story

I want you to pause for a moment and imagine something with me.

Picture your life as a blank canvas. You are the painter, and God hands you a brush. He says, **"Paint a picture of your life right now."**

What would it look like? Would it be filled with bright colors or covered in shadows? Would it show joy, peace, and purpose or pain, confusion, and disappointment?

Now ask yourself: **Are you really holding the brush?** Or have you handed it to someone else?

Too often, we allow others to paint our story. We let people's opinions, expectations, and judgments define us. But the problem is **they can't see what God sees**. They only see through their own broken lens. And when we give away our brush, we give them control over our identity, our choices, and our future.

I had to ask myself, **why would I let someone else write my story when God already has?** He's the Author of life **(Hebrews 12:2)**, the One who knows the end from the beginning **(Isaiah 46:10)**. He calls us His workmanship, His masterpiece **(Ephesians 2:10)**.

But so many of us live beneath that truth. We carry a weight God never asked us to carry, trying to please people, prove our worth, and chase approval. And when things don't go as planned; the job falls through, the relationship ends, the dream delays, we don't hear comfort. We hear criticism. We hear lies.

But lies don't define us. God does.

Take Job, for example. He lost everything: his family, his health, his possessions. His friends assumed it was his fault. His own wife told him to curse God and die **(Job 2:9)**. Imagine if he had listened to them. What if he had handed them the brush?

But Job held on to God. And because of that, his story didn't end in ashes, it ended in restoration **(Job 42:10)**.

I know what it feels like because I've lived it too.

When I was younger, I didn't understand who I was or what would become of my life. I searched for meaning in people, places, and things, hoping they could define my worth. But all it brought me was emptiness, and some of the loneliest moments of my life.

Still, deep down, I knew there was something different about me. Something only God could reveal.

People who didn't know me or my story told me I'd never amount to anything. And for a while, I believed them. I could've kept living under their labels, running with someone else's narrative about me. But then **God found me**. I wasn't even looking for Him, but He showed up anyway.

And when He did, He started whispering truth over my life. He told me about the plans He had for me. He opened my eyes. He showed me that I was His… that I was chosen. And from that moment on, I knew only **God** had the right to tell my story.

Here's the truth: You weren't made by people. You were made by God. And like any good designer, He knows how you're supposed to function.

Think about a car. It doesn't know it's a car. It relies on its designer and its manual. When something breaks, you don't just take it anywhere, you take it to the manufacturer or a trained mechanic.

Why would you treat your soul any differently?

God made you. His Word is your manual. His Spirit is your guide. Stop handing your story to people who didn't create you. Stop chasing approval from those who didn't call you. God already has.

"You are fearfully and wonderfully made." – Psalm 139:14
"You are chosen, holy, and dearly loved." – Colossians 3:12
"You are more than a conqueror through Him who loves you." – Romans 8:37

People may mean well, but they don't have the final say. God does. And one of the most beautiful things about Him? He loves you completely, unconditionally, and nothing can change that **(Romans 8:38–39)**.

So today, take back your brush.

Don't let your life be defined by others. Don't live stuck in someone else's version of your story. Let God guide your hand as you paint boldly, brightly, and beautifully.

Even if the road feels dark, He's still with you. Even if you've been waiting for answers, He's still working. But you won't see His light if you keep your eyes on the shadows.

Let His truth guide your vision. Let His Word be the paint for your masterpiece.

Because you are His masterpiece. Not because I said so, but because **He** did.

Pray with me

Father,

I thank You for every person reading this right now. I pray You'd remind them of who they are in You. Break off every lie they've believed. Silence the voices that speak death, and release Your truth that brings life. Show them that their story isn't over, and that You are still writing it. Give them the courage to take back the brush and let You lead. Thank You for loving us unconditionally, for calling us chosen, and for never leaving us. We trust You with our story.

In Jesus' name,
Amen.

Day 8

You Are Priceless:
See Yourself Through God's Eyes

I was watching a YouTube video today, and a young boy asked his mother, **"How much is my life worth?"**

Instead of answering, she handed him a stone and said, "Go out and find how much this is worth. When you're done, come back, and I'll answer your question."

So the boy went out and asked three different people.

The first man looked at the stone and said, **"I'm not sure, but I'll give you a piece of fruit for it."**
The second man glanced at it and replied, **"I don't need one of those."**

But the third man's eyes lit up. He said, **"This is the most perfect gem I've ever seen. I can't even imagine its value. In my opinion, it's priceless."**

The boy returned home, still confused, and asked, **"Mom, what does this stone have to do with the value of my life?"**

She looked at him and said, **"People will value you based on their point of view, their level of information, and their** belief in you. But that doesn't change the fact that you are priceless. Remember, surround yourself with people who value you."

Let that sink in. **You are priceless.** Not because of how people see you, but because of how **God sees you**.

The Word of God says, *"I praise You because I am fearfully and wonderfully made; Your works are wonderful, I know that full well"* **(Psalm 139:14).** That's who you are fearfully, wonderfully, and purposefully made by God.

The following quote is one of my favorites. **"Everything we think comes into existence, so only think things that you want to come into existence. How you think creates how you feel. How you feel becomes an emotion. That emotion becomes a vibration. And that vibration becomes a magnet that attracts things to you. So protect your mind."**

Translation? Protect your mind. **Proverbs 4:23** reminds us, *"Above all else, guard your heart, for everything you do flows from it."* Be mindful of what you think about. Because what lives in your mind will eventually show up in your life.

Let me share something real with you. I was sitting in the living room after a long, draining day. The TV was on, but I wasn't really watching it. I was just tired, mentally, emotionally, all of it. Then my phone buzzed. It was a message from my daughter. Five simple words: **"You are a good dad."**

Those five words hit me deep. I'm not usually the emotional type, but my eyes filled with tears. In that moment, it felt like God was using her to say, **"I see you. I'm proud of you."**

Let this speak to you today: People who are truly sent by God to walk with you will never use their words as weapons.

They won't tear you down when you're already struggling. They won't make you feel small when you're trying to grow. They'll speak life. They'll call out the greatness in you, even when you can't see it for yourself. **But even if no one else ever does, God already has.**

He saw value in you before you ever proved anything. **Romans 5:8** says, *"But God demonstrates His own love for us in this: While we were still sinners, Christ died for us."*

That's priceless. You are priceless. Stop letting every opinion become your identity. Just because someone says you're not enough doesn't mean it's true. What does God say? **He says you're chosen (1 Peter 2:9), loved (Jeremiah 31:3), and created with purpose (Ephesians 2:10).**

Stop shrinking to fit into what others expect from you. It's time to stand firm in the truth of who God made you to be. Sometimes, God doesn't clear the fog around you; instead, He gives you wings to rise above it.

Hear this deep in your spirit today: You are good enough. You are deeply loved. You are fully seen. You are chosen. You are priceless.

There will be times when you feel invisible, like no one notices the burdens you carry or the fight inside you. But God does. He never sleeps. He never forgets. He never overlooks those He calls His own.

Isaiah 49:16 says, *"See, I have engraved you on the palms of my hands."*

Stop people-pleasing. That's called survival mode, but you're stepping into revival mode now. You're stepping into your

God-given purpose. And anyone truly meant to walk with you will never ask you to dim your light just to make them feel safe.

The enemy will try to distract you with lies, delays, and doubts. Don't fall for it. Keep your eyes fixed on God. Keep your faith strong. **Philippians 1:6** reminds us, *"He who began a good work in you will carry it on to completion until the day of Christ Jesus."*

Just like that stone the boy was asked to value, your life is priceless; not because I say it, but because God says it. No one else can put a price on your worth. People might try, but only God truly knows the treasure you are. **He made you fearfully and wonderfully, loved you before you even took your first breath, and sealed your value with His own blood on the cross.**

So hold this truth close: you are priceless, chosen, and deeply loved. When the world tries to tell you otherwise, remember who declares you are enough, God's truth does. And His truth is the only thing that truly matters.

Pray with me

Father God,

Thank You for creating me with divine intention. Thank You for calling me priceless, even when the world tries to put a price tag on me. Remind me to silence every lie and align my heart with Your truth. Let me walk boldly in my purpose, unapologetically whole and fully seen by You. May I never forget that my identity comes from You, not from people pleasing, titles, or validation. Use my life for Your glory.

In Jesus' name, Amen.

Day 9

The Question That Could Change Everything

I want to ask you something. And I don't want you to answer right away. In fact, I hope you pause, reflect, and be completely honest; not with me, but with **yourself and with God**.

If you could ask God one question, and you knew He would answer you audibly, right now, what would you ask Him?

Take a moment to let that sink in. I did!

Don't ask your friend, your pastor, a co-worker, or even a family member. Don't try to hide it. This is about being real, honest, and completely transparent with **your Father**. The One who already knows what's inside of you, but invites you to speak anyway. Don't look for someone else's answer. **This is about your heart. Your question. Your voice.**

You may be wondering, **"Why that question?"**

Because I want you to feel the heart of God. I want you to recognize how deeply He loves you and how relentlessly He has pursued you, **not for religion, but for relationship.**

When God created the heavens and the earth, He looked at His creation and called it **good**. But He created Adam and Eve, flawless, blameless, without stain or wrinkle. They were His masterpiece. But they were deceived. Not by God, but by **an enemy whose only mission is to separate us from the One who made us.**

They believed a lie, and that lie led to separation. But even then, God began a redemption story that never stopped unfolding.

Sound familiar?

From the beginning, people have listened to the wrong voices. We've connected with the wrong spirits. We've chased temporary things and believed one lie after another. And yet, none of it stopped God from trying to bring us back.

When He delivered His people from Egypt, they complained and doubted, turning what could've been an 11-day journey into 40 years of wandering **(Exodus 16:2-3; Numbers 14:33-34)**. When they asked Samuel for a human king, God reminded him, *"They're not rejecting you, Samuel. They're rejecting Me, as they have from the beginning."* **(1 Samuel 8:7)**

And still, God keeps coming for you.

Even when Elijah stood on Mount Carmel and called down fire to reveal the one true God, the people only returned for a moment before drifting again **(1 Kings 18:21-39)**. And yet, God kept reaching.

Why? **Because His love is unfailing**.

"The Lord is compassionate and gracious, slow to anger, abounding in love." - **Psalm 103:8**

And then came the greatest act of love: God sent His Son, Jesus; not just to speak the truth, but to be the truth. To walk among us. To carry our pain. To pay the price for our sin. He endured betrayal, rejection, beatings, and death; not because we were worthy, but because He couldn't bear for us to be separated from Him.

Can you imagine sending your child into a world that would reject and crucify them, all for the sake of restoring someone who may still turn away? That's how deep God's love goes.

"But God demonstrates His own love for us in this: While we were still sinners, Christ died for us." - **Romans 5:8**

You see, Jesus came to restore what was lost. To erase shame, heal wounds, break chains, and reconnect you to the heart of your Father. And today, no matter where you've been or what you've done, you need to hear this: you are not too far gone.

"I have loved you with an everlasting love; I have drawn you with unfailing kindness." - **Jeremiah 31:3**

You're not forgotten. You haven't missed your chance. And there is absolutely nothing that can separate you from His love.

"I am convinced that neither death nor life, neither angels nor demons… nor anything else in all creation, will be able to separate us from the love of God that is in Christ Jesus our Lord." - **Romans 8:38–39**

So maybe your question for God is **about your past**. Or maybe it's **about your future**. Maybe it comes from **a place of deep pain or deep hope**. Whatever it is, **He's not afraid of it. He's not avoiding you**. He welcomes your questions because He's after your heart, not just your words.

Sometimes your question will lead you to answers. Sometimes it will lead you to a deeper relationship. Either way, if it brings you closer to Him, it's worth asking.

"Fear not, for I have redeemed you; I have called you by name; you are mine." - Isaiah 43:1

The more you lean into Him, the more your heart begins to beat with His. And as it does, your questions may start to change, not because they weren't valid, but because His love starts becoming the answer you never knew you needed.

So go ahead. Ask Him.

Ask in faith. Ask in honesty. Ask like a child who trusts that their Father is listening, because He is. And He always has been.

Pray with me

Father God,

Thank You for loving me even when I didn't understand it. Thank You for never turning away when I've had doubts, questions, and fears. Today, I come to You with an open heart. I bring my questions, my confusion, my longing, and I ask You to speak. Show me who You are. Let me feel Your love in a deeper way. Help me see that You've never left me, and You're not leaving now. I may not get all the answers, but remind me that You are the answer. I trust You. I belong to You.

In Jesus' name, Amen.

Day 10

Faith Over Fear: Your Are Ready

Let me talk to you for a minute; not as someone who has it all together, but as someone who knows what it's like to be unsure. Maybe you're in that place where you feel God is pulling you toward something different, something new, and it's stretching you. Maybe it's walking away from a job that's draining the life out of you, or stepping into a new opportunity that makes you nervous. Maybe you're trying to heal from something no one knows about, forgive someone who hurt you, or finally face a part of your life you've been avoiding. It could be going back to school, starting over in a new city, letting go of a relationship that isn't healthy, or simply choosing peace instead of chaos. Whatever it is, you feel it: that pull in your spirit, that gentle but firm voice saying, **"It's time."**

And here's the thing: it's normal to feel nervous. Life has a way of throwing moments at us that make us question everything. Fear creeps in, uncertainty holds us back, and we start wondering, **"Am I really ready for this?"** But I want to tell you something right now: **You are. You are ready.**

God doesn't call the qualified. He qualifies the called. He's been getting you ready, not in the way you imagined, but in the quiet moments, the difficult seasons, the times you didn't even realize He was preparing you. Every tear, every hard lesson, every prayer you said in the dark has been part of the process. It might feel like you're walking into the unfamiliar, but you're walking with the One who knows everything.

I remember the first time I was asked to speak in church after giving my life to Jesus. I was a nervous wreck for days, running through all the "what ifs." What if I sounded foolish? What if my message wasn't clear? What if I panicked? I was putting so much pressure on myself, forgetting that this wasn't about me, it was about God.

That morning, I sat in the back of the church completely overwhelmed as I watched the room fill up faster than I expected. My hands were shaky. My heart was racing. Then I felt a hand on my shoulder. It was the pastor.

"Are you ready?" he asked.

I opened my mouth to respond, but nothing came out. I wasn't sure if I was ready. I wasn't even sure what "ready" was supposed to feel like. My heart was pounding so hard it felt like everyone in the church could hear it, and then he led me to the front.

I walked up to a small wooden podium, adjusted the microphone, took a deep breath, introduced myself, and prayed these simple words: **"Let Your will be done."**

When I opened my eyes, I heard: **"Let Me use you for My glory."**

That's exactly what I did. I didn't let fear control me. That day, many people gave their lives to Christ, not because of great sounding words or a perfect delivery, but because of obedience. I stepped aside so God could shine.

Maybe right now, you're standing in front of something that feels too big. Maybe fear is making you hesitate. But let me remind you what's true: David didn't defeat Goliath through skill, but because he was willing. God was the force behind the stone **(1 Samuel 17:47)**. Moses didn't part the Red Sea. His faith did, and God made the way **(Exodus 14:21)**. Peter walked on water not by power, but by trusting Jesus. And when fear got a hold of him, he sank **(Matthew 14:29-31)**.

Faith isn't the absence of fear. It's the decision not to let fear lead. Greatness doesn't mean you won't be afraid. It means you'll move forward anyway.

When God calls you, whether the assignment is public or private, big or small, He's already prepared you. You don't have to be perfect. You don't have to be seasoned. You just have to be willing. Esther risked her life to go before the king and said, *"If I perish, I perish"* **(Esther 4:16)**. That wasn't weakness. That was bold, holy faith.

Sometimes no one else can help you; only God. Yes, friends and leaders are a gift, but when God gives the assignment, He is the One who will see it through. Stop trying to figure it all out. That's not your job. Your job is to walk forward, even if fear is still trying to hold you.

Fear and faith can exist in the same space, but only one can lead. Let faith speak louder. ***"If God is for us, who can be against us?"*** (**Romans 8:31**).

"Faith is being sure of what we hope for and certain of what we do not see." (**Hebrews 11:1**)

Greatness is waiting on your obedience. You got this, because God's got you. Now go.

Pray with me

Father God,

Thank You for calling me, for equipping me, and for choosing me. Even when fear tries to rise, let faith rise higher. Remind me that You are with me; that I never walk alone. Give me the courage to obey, the strength to endure, and the peace to know You are in control. I lay down my doubts, my excuses, and my fears. Have Your way in me. Use me for Your glory.

In Jesus' name,
Amen.

Day 11

You Are the Miracle

If you haven't already, I want to encourage you to start your day by **thanking God and spending time with Him**.

I don't know what your routine looks like…maybe it's prayer, reading your Bible, listening to worship music, sitting still in His presence, or simply talking to Him. However it happens, just make space for Him. It doesn't have to look like anyone else's time with God, **because He's not after a performance, He's after your presence.**

You don't have to pretend with God. You don't need to put on a mask. You don't need a title, a clean record, or a fancy prayer. Just show up **as you are**.

"Come to Me, all you who are weary and burdened, and I will give you rest." - **Matthew 11:28**

I want to remind you of something today, and I pray you really receive it: **God loves you**. And I mean really loves you. Not just in a general, distant way. He loves you specifically, right now, as you are.

You want to see a miracle?
Stand up. Walk to the nearest mirror. Look in it.
There it is: the miracle God made. It's you.

You've been praying for a breakthrough, for something to change, for a sign that you're on the right path. Let this be your sign: **you are not forgotten. You are the miracle in motion**.

You are also **one decision away** from stepping into the life God has been preparing for you. It starts with a choice; the moment you decide that you're ready to believe what God says about you is true.

If you're struggling to believe that, take a deep breath. Close your eyes. Picture your younger self. What would you tell them?

I'd tell mine: "**Don't be so hard on yourself. You're going to make mistakes, and it's okay. Learn from them. Forgive quickly. Love deeply. Be kind to yourself. And always trust God, especially when it feels like He's silent. Because He's not. He's listening. You're going to be okay.**"

Because here's the truth: You will have victories and failures. You'll win some and lose some. People will come and go. **But God will always remain.** He is the constant in a world full of change. He's the One whose love doesn't waver.

"Jesus Christ is the same yesterday, today, and forever."
- **Hebrews 13:8**

So stop measuring your worth by someone else's expectations. Stop letting people's opinions define your value. You don't need their validation when you already have **God's approval**.

You are not their label. You are God's masterpiece. ***"You are fearfully and wonderfully made."* - Psalm 139:14**

Today, stop beating yourself up because you don't fit into everyone's box. God never asked you to. You were **handpicked, set apart, and called by name**, and yes, that comes with a heavy assignment sometimes. Not everyone can walk the road you're called to… and that's okay.

When I think about God, the first word that comes to my heart is love, and then sacrifice.

Because that's what Jesus did. He loved you so much that He gave up everything to bring you back into relationship with the Father. **He went to the cross for you**, not just to save your soul, but so you could live **free**.

Free from guilt.
Free from shame.
Free from trying to be perfect.

***"So if the Son sets you free, you will be free indeed."* - John 8:36**

Don't ignore the gift. **Embrace it.** He gave His life so you could finally start living yours, healed, whole, forgiven, and full of purpose.

You were not made to just survive; **you were made to thrive in the freedom of His love**.

So today, walk in that freedom.

Smile. Breathe. Look in the mirror again and say it out loud:
"I am loved. I am chosen. I am a miracle. I am God's."

Pray with me

Heavenly Father,

Thank You for waking me up this morning. Thank You for loving me, even when I struggle to love myself. Thank You for calling me worthy when I've called myself unqualified. Forgive me for the times I've doubted my value. Forgive me for comparing, hiding, or pretending. Today, I choose to believe Your truth over every lie.

Help me to see myself the way You see me. fearfully and wonderfully made, chosen, loved, and called. Remind me that I'm not just trying to make it through life… I'm walking out a purpose that You designed before I was even born.

Thank You, Jesus, for going to the cross for me. Thank You for breaking every chain, tearing every wall down, and making a way for me to live free. I receive Your love. I receive Your grace. I receive the life You died to give me. Today, I will walk in it.

In Jesus' name, Amen.

Day 12

The Power of Telling God the Truth

If you've ever smiled in public while falling apart in private, **this is for you**.

If you've ever held back tears because you didn't think anyone would understand, you're not the only one. Life can hit hard; mentally, emotionally, spiritually, and sometimes it just feels too personal to put into words, let alone share with anyone .

But if there's one thing I know for sure, it's this: **God is still good.**

And He sees you. He hears you. And He cares more than you know.

June is National Men's Mental Health Awareness Month, and while it shines a light on what many men struggle with quietly, the truth is, **it's a conversation that matters for all of us**. Whether you're a man or a woman, we've all had moments where we smiled on the outside but battled silently on the inside.

I saw a video the other day where a group of men were asked a simple question: **"Who do you call when you're at your lowest?"** Almost every man gave the same answer: **"No one."** That stuck with me. I had to pause and ask myself, who do I turn to when I feel like I'm slipping? And if the answer is no one, why is that?

Is it fear of being misunderstood? Or maybe you're tired of feeling like a burden to everyone. Maybe you've told yourself, **"No one would really get it anyway, or who would care?"** But that's not true.

You may be in a moment right now where you're running on empty. You're doing your best to show up for everyone, but inside, something's breaking. I want you to hear me clearly: you're not weak for feeling tired. You're not broken because you need help. And you're not less of a person for admitting that you're struggling.

God cares. He hears the words you're too afraid to say out loud. He sees every battle you're fighting in secret, and He's not turning away from you. He's drawing closer.

In **1 Samuel 1**, Hannah was in deep pain. She longed for a child and couldn't take the quiet anymore. She went to the temple, **poured out her soul, and prayed from a place only God could understand**. Her husband meant well, but he didn't really get it. Eli the priest saw her and assumed she was drunk. **But God didn't misunderstand her**. He heard her cry and gave her a son that she named Samuel, which means **heard by God**. Her pain turned into purpose, and her tears became part of a greater story.

Hannah didn't wait for permission to be honest about what she was going through. She didn't wait for someone else to validate her pain. **She just took it to God. And He met her right where she was**, and He will do the same for you.

You don't have to hold it all in. You don't have to pretend you're doing well when it feels like your whole world is crumbling around you. You don't have to carry the pressure of being strong for everyone else, anymore. God is inviting you to bring it all to Him. And guess what? **You can trust Him**.

The Bible says, *"Cast all your anxiety on Him because He cares for you"* **(1 Peter 5:7)**. Not just some of it. Not just the parts you think are acceptable. **All of it**.

David understood this too. Just look at the Psalms. **He cried out, he questioned, he worshiped, and through it all, God never turned him away.**

Even Jesus, the Son of God, knelt in the Garden of Gethsemane and said, *"My soul is overwhelmed with sorrow…"* **(Matthew 26:38)**. His friends fell asleep while He was in agony, but the Father never left Him.

You don't have to wait until you got it all together. You don't have to clean up your prayers or edit your emotions. **Just be real with God. He's not afraid of your truth. He's already seen the worst and still loves you with the best.**

As you learn to be honest with God, don't forget, there are people around you who are fighting their own silent battles. They may not need someone to fix them. They just need someone who won't judge them. Someone who will listen. **Be that**

safe place for someone. And remember this: **God is that safe place for you, always**.

If you feel unseen, He sees you. If you feel unheard, He's listening. If you feel like you're slipping, He's still holding on.

You are never alone. Just like God told Joshua, He promises to be with you wherever you go. So take heart, be strong and courageous. Don't let fear or discouragement win, because the Lord your God is right there with you, every step, every moment (**Joshua 1:9**). Lean into that truth. Hold on to it like your life depends on it, because sometimes, it does.

Pray with me

Father God,

Thank You for always being near. Thank You for listening when no one else seems to understand. Today, I bring You the parts of me I've kept hidden. The questions, the fear, the exhaustion. I know You're not afraid of my truth. Heal what hurts. Restore what's worn down. And remind me again that I'm never alone. You are my safe place.

In Jesus' name,
Amen.

Day 13

Today, I Give You Your Flowers

You may not know this yet… **but today is sacred**. Not because it's a holiday. Not because something big is happening. **But because God has something to say to you, right now**.

This is a moment. A divine interruption. A personal letter from Heaven, disguised as a few paragraphs on your screen. And it's not about me: it's all about **you**. Because **God sees you**, and today, He wants you to know that.

Too many people wait to say the things that matter most; to give the encouragement, the appreciation, the **"thank you"** that someone's heart is aching to hear. **But not today. Today, I want to give you your flowers, while you can still hold them**. While you're still standing. Still pushing. Still believing, even when no one else knows how much it's cost you.

We live in a world where strangers are praised for their fame, their beauty, or their platform, yet the people right beside us are overlooked. People like **you**, who sacrifice daily, who carry burdens in silence, who stay up late to pray for others, who give when no one gives back, who smile even while holding back tears.

This is for you: not just for a certain kind of person, but for every kind. Maybe you're a single parent holding your family together. Maybe you're the friend who always checks on others, even when you're struggling yourself. Maybe you're carrying responsibilities that no one sees. Or maybe you're just trying to make it through the day, hoping someone notices you're still here.

Whoever you are, this is for you. Because God sees you. God hears you. God knows.

"The LORD is close to the brokenhearted and saves those who are crushed in spirit." – **Psalm 34:18**

Even if the people you're sacrificing for haven't noticed, **God has**.
Even if no one says "thank you," **God does**.
Even if the world scrolls past your pain, **He never does**.

"God is not unjust; He will not forget your work and the love you have shown Him as you have helped His people." – **Hebrews 6:10**

Maybe you've been overlooked. Maybe you've been carrying more than you let on. You've encouraged others, but no one checks on you. You've prayed for people, but feel like your own prayers go unheard. You've put yourself last; not out of weakness, but out of love.

And God saw it all. Every quiet act of faith. Every late-night cry. Every time you didn't give up.

"The eyes of the LORD are on the righteous, and His ears are attentive to their cry." - **Psalm 34:15**

So today, I celebrate you. I applaud you. And if no one has told you lately: you matter. **Especially to God**.

You don't need a title. You don't need a perfect life. You don't need to be known by the world. God doesn't choose people based on outer appearances. He looks at the heart.

"People look at the outward appearance, but the LORD looks at the heart." - **1 Samuel 16:7**

You are f**earfully and wonderfully made**. Handcrafted by the Creator of the universe. You don't have to come to Him polished. You don't have to fake it. You just have to come as you are.

"Come to Me, all you who are weary and burdened, and I will give you rest." - **Matthew 11:28**

And the best part? **Jesus went to the cross because He loves you.** Because He wanted you to know **His Father**, and to walk in the fullness of who you were created to be. No person, no mistake, no past can cancel the purpose God placed inside you.

"For I am convinced that neither death nor life… nor anything else in all creation, will be able to separate us from the love of God that is in Christ Jesus our Lord." - **Romans 8:38–39**

God told me to write this today to remind you: **He hasn't forgotten about you.** He sees the seeds you've sown in tears.

He knows the nights you almost quit. And He's saying, **"Hold on - I'm not finished with your story."**

"For I know the plans I have for you," declares the Lord, "plans to prosper you and not to harm you, plans to give you a hope and a future." - **Jeremiah 29:11**

So before today ends, I want you to do something. Get up. Find a mirror. Look at yourself and **smile**. Then say these words out loud: **"I am amazing. I am loved. God sees me. And He's not finished with me yet."**

Because it's true.

Pray with me

Father God,

Thank You for seeing me, even when I feel invisible. Thank You for loving me, even when I feel unworthy. Thank You for carrying me, even when I didn't have the strength to stand.

Help me to rest in Your presence and remember that I don't have to perform to be loved by You. Remind me that I matter not because of what I do, but because of who I am in You. Let Your peace cover me, and Your purpose stir within me again. Use my life to bring You glory. And when I forget who I am, remind me that I am Yours.

In Jesus' name,
Amen.

Day 14

Stay on Your Post

No matter what's going on in your life: big storms or quiet struggles, God says, **"Stay on your post."**

When people talk about you, twist your words, or try to drag your name through the mud, don't flinch. Stay right where He planted you. Their words don't define you. They were never yours to carry.

If I got a dime for every negative thing said about me, I'd give it away because those words don't belong to me. The same goes for the things spoken about you. They only affect you if you choose to believe them. **Don't accept things that God never gave you.**

Here's something the Holy Spirit had to teach me the hard way: what people think of you is none of your business. That's their burden, not yours.

If people call you names, misunderstand you, or misjudge your intentions, don't take it personally. What they say is a reflection of how they see you, not who you truly are. Let their opinions fade away like smoke in the wind. You are made in the image of God, and that's who you are.

Jesus said, *"If the world hates you, remember it hated Me first"* (**John 15:18**). And yet, He still went to the Cross. Still loved. Still forgave. Still stayed on His post.

Let that sink in.

People misunderstood Him. They mocked Him. Lied about Him. Betrayed Him. But He never wavered. He had a mission. And so do you.

Some people will leave your life, and it may be difficult. But let them go. Don't chase after what God is trying to remove. A new season is coming, and not everyone is meant to go with you. It's not rejection; it's just God moving you in a new direction.

When God calls you higher, He'll often call you into a quiet place. A place where it's just you and Him. Yes, it might feel lonely, but it's holy ground. In that solitude, He's shaping you, stretching you, and filling you with strength for the call on your life.

"Be still, and know that I am God." (**Psalm 46:10**)

You don't have to fight every battle. You don't have to defend yourself when people misunderstand. Trust God with the chaos. One minute people will cheer you on. The next, they'll talk behind your back like you were never part of their story.

Don't strike back. Don't let bitterness grow roots in your heart. **Love like Jesus**. Forgive like Jesus. Walk away if you must; but walk away clean.

Remember, the enemy is the accuser. He's been doing this since the beginning; day and night. But *"There is no condemnation for those who are in Christ Jesus"* (**Romans 8:1**). You are not what they say. You are who He says.

God has placed people in your life who are meant to stay and walk with you. The real ones don't walk away when things get difficult. They pray for you, stand by you, and believe with you.

And if you're reading this feeling like there's no light at the end of the tunnel, hear me: **You are the light.** God placed you here to reflect His Son. So shine; especially when darkness tries to shut you down.

Stay on your post. Let your life shine like a light, pointing others to His glory.

Pray with me

Father God,

Thank You for seeing us, choosing us, and placing us where we are for such a time as this. Help us to stay faithful, even when it's hard. Help us to shake off the words that don't come from You and cling to what You've spoken. Fill us with the boldness of Jesus and the gentleness of His love. Teach us to rest in Your presence and trust Your timing. Keep our hearts soft and our spirits strong. May our lives reflect Your glory. We don't want the spotlight, only Your light.

In Jesus' name,
Amen.

Day 15

What Kind of Net Are You

Before you keep scrolling, can you pause for a second? Take a deep breath. Now ask yourself this, and really think about it: **What kind of net are you?**

It's not just about what you say, it's about your spirit. Not just how you look on the outside, but how you show up for others. Because the truth is, people around you are slipping, and they're hoping someone, anyone, will be there to catch them before they hit the ground.

Some nets look big and impressive, but they're full of holes, so they don't catch much of anything. Some are strong, but they're tangled up in pride. And some started out pure, but over time, bitterness and hurt wore them down. But then there are those rare nets, held together by prayer, humility, and real love. The kind that catch what others drop. The kind that hold what others can't carry. The kind that don't just help, but gently lead people straight to the heart of God.

God is asking today: **What kind of net are you?**

We live in a world where a lot of people don't know how to fall without getting hurt. We say, "How are you?" but rarely listen for the truth behind the answer. A lot of people are falling apart on the inside—hiding behind smiles, polite answers, and silent struggles. Yes, they should cast their cares on Jesus. But before they do, many cast them toward us, hoping we'll care enough to catch them.

"Cast all your anxiety on Him, because He cares for you."
-1 Peter 5:7

But can He trust you to care, too?

My daughter knows this one thing: when she comes to me, she's safe. She can speak without fear. She can cry without shame. She can be fully seen and still fully loved. Why? Because I don't try to fix her. I just show up for her. I listen. I'm there for her when things are tough, and I cheer her on when things go well. She knows she can always come to me: I'm her safe place.

That's what the world is aching for.

When was the last time someone opened up to you, and you didn't preach, but you listened? When was the last time someone opened up around you; not met with judgment or advice, but simply met with the love of Jesus?

Some people don't need a sermon. They need a safe space.

Jesus called us to be fishers of men, to go and make disciples of all nations, but He also showed us how to love them well. It's not just about casting the net far and wide; it's about making sure it's strong enough to carry people with compassion, grace, and truth.

"Come, follow me," Jesus said, "and I will send you out to fish for people." - Matthew 4:19

The kind of net you are determines what you catch, what you carry, and what you point people toward.

This isn't just about kindness, it's kingdom. This is about love that bears all things. This is about patience that doesn't rush healing. This is about listening as an act of spiritual warfare: standing between a soul and the lie that says, **"no one cares."**

"Be completely humble and gentle; be patient, bearing with one another in love." - Ephesians 4:2

And yes, this is about right now. Because today, people are drowning silently, scrolling, hoping, whispering, **"God, send someone."**

Maybe that someone is **you**.

Maybe the person who seems the strongest is carrying the heaviest weight. Maybe the friend who always makes you laugh is breaking behind closed doors. Maybe God placed you in their life not to fix them, not to preach at them, but simply to be the net.

A net that catches. A net that listens. A net that loves without condition and holds without breaking.

"Carry each other's burdens, and in this way you will fulfill the law of Christ." - Galatians 6:2

So again I ask you: **What kind of net are you?**

The world may be chasing attention, influence, and applause, but heaven's looking for hearts that carry God's glory, hold onto truth, move with real compassion, and quietly show the love of Jesus in everyday ways.

So, **what kind of net are you**? Are you someone who catches others with grace, or are you in need of being caught yourself? No matter where you are, the invitation is the same: let God be your net, and let Him use you to be a net for others.

Don't wait for the perfect moment: step into your purpose today. Be the net. Reach out with compassion. And if you need someone to catch you, know that God's love is always there.

Pray with me

Father God,

Make me a net that catches what others have dropped. A net that holds the heavy things without breaking. A net that points people not to me, but to You. Take the frayed pieces of my heart and mend them with grace. Make me gentle. Make me patient. Make me safe, not soft, not silent, but safe. Holy Spirit, help me to listen well, love well, carry well, and reflect Jesus in how I show up for the broken and burdened. I don't just want to speak truth, I want to live it. May the net of my life be soaked in Your presence and stretched wide by Your love.

In Jesus' name,
Amen.

This Is Not a Dress Rehearsal

When I was in sixth grade, I auditioned for and was given a starring role in a school play. I'm not entirely sure what made me want to try out, but I went for it. For months, I memorized my lines, practiced with the cast, and learned how to manage the responsibility that came with a leading role. During the dress rehearsal; the final run-through before the big day, everything clicked. We were focused, we were ready, and it felt just right.

On the day of the performance, my nerves hit hard. I looked out at the audience and spotted my classmates, and just like that, the pressure felt heavier. But even with the butterflies in my stomach, I knew I was ready. I had practiced. I knew my part. **The only thing that could stop me now, was me**. Then, my drama teacher looked me in the eyes and spoke life into me. It might have seemed like a small moment, but something shifted deep inside. It was a quiet, powerful turning point I'd never forget.

So why am I sharing this story? Because life isn't a play, and there are no do-overs. This is your moment. Your opportunity to show up and **shine for God**.

Sometimes, God will call you to step into something that feels completely outside your comfort zone. Something that doesn't seem to match your experience, your personality, or your plans. You might wonder, **"Why me?"** especially when others seem more qualified, more confident, more ready. But if you're not careful, fear, comparison, and the wrong voices will talk you out of what God has already confirmed.

David wasn't trained for battle, but he ran straight toward Goliath with nothing but a sling and faith. Peter didn't walk on water because of ability. He stepped out because he trusted Jesus. Joshua wasn't a seasoned leader when he took Moses' place, but he moved forward with a single promise from God and a heart fully surrendered.

Unlike the play I participated in, life isn't a rehearsal. There's no practice round, no second take. **This is real. This is purpose. This is Kingdom assignment.** You can't keep waiting for the stars to align, for the timing to feel safe, or for others to validate what God already confirmed. When God says "Go," you don't need another opinion. Obedience is your permission.

"Before I formed you in the womb, I knew you; before you were born, I set you apart..." - **Jeremiah 1:5**

So if you've been hesitating; telling yourself you're not ready, not good enough, not equipped, **this is your wake-up call**. The dream, the idea, the **calling** you've been sitting on isn't waiting for another confirmation. It's waiting for your **yes**. This is your moment, and **God has already gone before you**.

When Paul encountered Jesus on the road to Damascus, everything changed. After being blinded and then healed, he didn't wait for comfort; he stepped into purpose.

Jesus, even as a young boy, was already walking in alignment with His Father's will. He didn't wait for a platform, applause, or permission. He didn't delay purpose for comfort. **He moved when the Father said move.** Because when God sends you, **excuses lose their power and timing**.

"Have I not commanded you? Be strong and courageous. Do not be afraid; do not be discouraged, for the Lord your God will be with you wherever you go." **- Joshua 1:9**

So what's stopping you? What are you waiting for? What has God called you to that you've buried under fear, excuses, or delays?

Maybe you feel like Peter, sinking in shame. Or like Elijah, overwhelmed and hiding in the dark. Maybe you feel like Moses, standing before an impossible sea with nothing but a word. **But the same God who met them in their breaking point will meet you in yours.** He didn't wait until they were confident. **He moved when they chose to trust.**

"Faith without works is dead." **- James 2:26**

The truth is, faith doesn't make fear go away; it just refuses to let fear control you. Faith says, **"Even if I don't feel ready, I'll still move forward because God is with me."** You don't have to be perfect, you just need to be willing. **You don't need to know every step; just take the first one.**

"The One who calls you is faithful, and He will do it." **- 1 Thessalonians 5:24**

God isn't asking you to perform or try to impress others. He's calling you to obey Him. He doesn't care about people's opinions; He wants you to glorify Him with your life. **Yes, following God's call will challenge you. Yes, it will cost you something.** But the reward of living with purpose and in sync with your Creator will be far greater than anything you give up.

Now is not the time to hold back. It's not the time to wait for others to approve. This is your moment to rise up and step into your calling.

No more practicing. No more doubting. No more waiting. **Now is the time to say yes.**

Pray with me

Lord,

I surrender every excuse, every fear, every delay. I know You've called me, not because I'm perfect, but because I'm Yours. Help me to stop rehearsing and start walking. I give You my full yes, not for my glory, but for Yours alone. Thank You for trusting me with purpose. Thank You for equipping me when I feel unqualified. Now, help me to move boldly, humbly, and fully surrendered.

In Jesus' name,
Amen.

Day 17

Permission to Prioritize You

Have you ever found yourself standing at the back of your own line?

It sounds strange, doesn't it? But maybe, like me, you've spent so much time showing up for everyone else, meeting their needs, supporting their dreams, wiping their tears, that you've forgotten what it feels like to show up for **you**. And on the rare occasion you do? Guilt tries to creep in like a shadow, whispering, **"You're being selfish."**

Let me tell you what a wise friend once told me: **"Every time you place others in front of you, without ever caring for yourself, you're pushing yourself further behind in your own line."**

That hit me hard. Because truthfully, when was the last time someone asked you how you're doing? When was the last time someone checked in on **you** without needing anything in return? It's not that we serve to be seen, or love to be praised. But let's be honest; kindness, when given back, can refresh a tired soul.

"Come to me, all who are weary and burdened, and I will give you rest." - Matthew 11:28

Too many of us are walking around emotionally drained, spiritually dry, and silently battling burdens no one sees. You give and give, until your cups runs dry, and there's nothing left to pour. And still, you hesitate to take time for yourself, afraid that choosing you will make you look ungrateful or weak. But let me say this in love and truth: **You are not weak for needing rest. You are not selfish for needing care. And you are not wrong for choosing you.**

God has placed a divine calling on your life: a purpose uniquely yours. Yes, helping others matters. Yes, showing up for people is beautiful. But not at the expense of your own soul. How can you pour living water into others when your own well is dry?

There's a line in a movie I once watched: *Morris Chestnut* was sitting outside, and someone asked him a question that stopped me cold: **"You take care of everyone... but who's taking care of you?"**

I couldn't answer that at the time. I looked for that answer in people, in accomplishments, in approval, but it wasn't until God called me to Himself that I understood. He showed me that the care I longed for wasn't found in others: **it was found in Him**. He reminded me that **He** is the One who fills the void, heals the heart, and strengthens the weary.

"The Lord will guide you always; He will satisfy your needs in a sun-scorched land and will strengthen your frame." - Isaiah 58:11

Even Jesus, perfect, sinless, all-powerful, faced this. People came to Him constantly. For healing. For help. For miracles. But how many came just to sit with Him, to care for Him, to ask how He was? In His darkest hour, even His closest followers scattered. And yet, He didn't fall apart. He went to the Father. His strength wasn't in the crowd, it was in His connection.

And for those of you reading this, that's your strength too.

Maybe your mission right now is drawing closer to God. Maybe it's starting the business He placed on your heart, returning to school, leaving that relationship that no longer honors Him, or simply learning to rest without guilt. Whatever it is, don't let shame, fear, or people-pleasing keep you from moving forward.

"Let us throw off everything that hinders and the sin that so easily entangles, and let us run with perseverance the race marked out for us." - **Hebrews 12:1**

Saying yes to God doesn't mean the road will be easy. It just means it'll be **worth it**. You may still face challenges, but you'll face them with clarity. With peace. With power. Because you're no longer running on empty.

Today, I encourage you to choose you. Not from a place of pride, but from a place of obedience. Your body, your heart, your spirit: it all belongs to God. Taking care of yourself is a responsibility. **It honors the God who made you.**

So pause. Breathe. Let go of the guilt. Say yes to the healing. Say yes to the calling. Say yes to rest, renewal, and redemption.

Because you matter. And you are not forgotten.

"You are God's masterpiece, created in Christ Jesus to do good works, which God prepared in advance for you to do."
- Ephesians 2:10

Pray with me

Father God,

Thank You for seeing me when I feel invisible. For reminding me that I am allowed to rest, to be restored, and to walk in purpose without guilt. Help me release every burden I was never meant to carry. Teach me to say yes to the things You've called me to, even when it means saying no to everyone else. I trust You to care for me as I learn to care for myself in a way that honors You. I surrender the guilt, the fear, and the pressure. Help me walk forward in grace, peace, and freedom.

In Jesus' name,
Amen.

You Are Not Forgotten: God Sees You

Guess what? If no one has told you lately, let me be the one to remind you: **You are amazing.** Your life has meaning, and it's not by accident. God knew you before you were formed in your mother's womb **(Jeremiah 1:5). You are a blessing, even if no one else sees it yet.**

Think about this: Yesterday is gone, never to be seen again. Tomorrow is uncertain, and if we're blessed to see it, praise God. **But today—today is a gift, a holy opportunity to glorify the One who gave you breath.**

So, what's been taking up space in your mind lately? Is it peace and joy? Or fear, loneliness, anxiety? **Be honest with yourself.** Sometimes, we suppress our pain and forget we were never meant to carry it alone.

For a long time, I didn't realize how much I was struggling. I felt lost: unseen, uncertain, unsure of my worth. I thought that if I worked harder, made more money, or followed the "expected" path, I'd finally find peace. But peace never came. I was always chasing something just out of reach.

It wasn't until God called me to step into His light that everything changed. I thought I had it all together. I heard sermons, motivational talks, and convinced myself I was on the right track. But deep down, I realized I was **where I wanted to be, not where God wanted me to be**. That's when God opened my eyes to His truth about my life. It was my own "**Damascus Road**" moment, like Saul before he became Paul.

In that moment, God showed me who I was, not just to give me identity, but to reveal who He was. I stepped out in faith, and though it wasn't easy or immediate, peace began to fill the spaces I had been trying to fill with the wrong things. I realized God had been waiting for me to knock, to seek Him with my whole heart.

Maybe you're feeling like I did, carrying a burden you weren't meant to bear, unsure of what's next, or if anyone sees you. You may feel stuck, wondering if anything will ever change. But I'm here to tell you: You're not alone. **God is waiting for you to ask, to seek, to knock on His door.** He's ready to show you a love and peace that only He can provide.

Jesus tells a powerful story in **Luke 11:5–13** about a man who knocked on his friend's door at midnight asking for bread. At first, the friend didn't respond, but because the man kept knocking, he eventually received what he needed. **This is how God wants us to come to Him; with bold, persistent faith.** He may not answer right away, but that doesn't mean He isn't listening. He's waiting to see if you'll keep knocking. As Jesus said in **Matthew 7:7**, *"Ask and it will be given to you; seek and you will find; knock and the door will be opened to you."* These aren't just words: they're promises.

So ask, not with hesitation, but with confidence. Seek, not the world, but the Kingdom. Knock, and trust that the right doors will open in God's perfect timing.

People may let you down. Life may break your heart. But God? He never will. His love is unconditional. His grace is unshakable. His promises are unchanging. When everyone else disappears, He is still right there.

Your relationship with God is the **most important** connection you'll ever have. No one will love you like He does. No one will sacrifice like Jesus did. No one will stay with you through the storm like the Holy Spirit will. ***"I will never leave you nor forsake you,"* He promised, and He meant it.**

So today, make a choice.
Ask.
Seek.
Knock.
And let God in.

He's been waiting for you: ready to pour out love, to lift your burdens, and to remind you that you are His: deeply loved, eternally valued, and completely seen.

Pray with me

Father God,

Thank You for seeing me; truly seeing me. I surrender my worries, my doubts, and my fears to You today. I ask for Your strength, Your guidance, and Your peace. I choose today to knock, to seek, and to ask. Help me walk in the confidence of knowing that I am Your child, that I am loved beyond measure, and that I am never alone.

In Jesus' name,
Amen.

Day 19

Don't Give Up: God's Just Getting Started

Whatever you do, no matter how hard the road gets, **don't you dare give up:** not on yourself, and definitely not on the dream God placed in your heart. I know it's been tough. Maybe you've been praying for weeks... months... even years. And still, the answer hasn't come. Still, the door hasn't opened. Still, you're staring at the sky wondering, **God, do You see me**?

But hear this: **keep moving forward**.

There will be people who don't see what you see. And that's okay, because the dream isn't theirs. It was never meant for their vision. God gave it to **YOU**. Some people can't support what they don't understand. They'll doubt you. Dismiss you. Even discourage you.

But let them. Because they're not the author of your story: **God is.**

"Being confident of this, that He who began a good work in you will carry it on to completion until the day of Christ Jesus." - Philippians 1:6

Take Joseph, for example. He shared his dream with his brothers, thinking they'd celebrate. Instead, jealousy blinded them, and they threw him into a pit. Can you imagine that? Looking up from that dark place, crying, confused, betrayed. But even then: **God had a plan.**

Joseph went from the pit, to being sold, to serving in Potiphar's house, where God's favor followed him. But just when things started to look up, the enemy came swinging. He was falsely accused and thrown into prison. Again, **he could've given up**. But God wasn't done. And even in the prison: **God was positioning him for the palace.**

So maybe right now, you feel like Joseph. Forgotten. Isolated. Maybe you're crying out from your own kind of pit. But hear me: **God hasn't forgotten you. He's forming you.** That dream you carry? It's still alive. And it's still possible.

"And we know that in all things God works for the good of those who love Him, who have been called according to His purpose." - Romans 8:28

It started when Joseph opened his mouth and shared what God showed him: but remember, not everyone can handle your vision. That doesn't mean you're wrong. That doesn't mean it's not from God. It just means **you've been called to something greater.**

I remember walking into a church once, just planning to meet with one of the church leaders. But before I even got to her, a woman teaching a class looked me in the eye and said something that changed everything:

"Stop trying to fit in. Let God place you."

Wait what? That hit me like a left hook. And maybe that's a word for you too. Maybe you've been forcing things: jobs, friendships, opportunities; trying to make something happen on your own. But God is strategic. When He shifts you, **it's not rejection, it's redirection**.

"A person's heart plans his way, but the Lord determines his steps." - **Proverbs 16:9**

You might think you're on the right road. You might feel like everything's lining up. And then, bam: God shifts everything. But guess what? **You're still right on schedule. God's schedule.**

When He removes something, it's because He's making room. When He isolates you, it's to quiet the noise so you can hear **Him**. The shift isn't punishment. It's preparation.

So don't panic when things don't go as planned. Don't fear being alone. God is repositioning you. He's protecting the promise inside of you. And just like Joseph, what the enemy meant for harm: **God will turn for good.**

And here's something important: You don't have to tell everyone everything. Some things are sacred. Some things are just between you and God. Protect the promise. Guard what God put in your heart

When Joseph finally came face to face with his brothers: the ones who betrayed him, he forgave them. And then he **blessed** them. That's what walking with God looks like. **It's not about revenge. It's about restoration.**

Let me keep it real: I'm not perfect. I don't have all the answers. But I trust God. Even when I don't understand the **"how,"** I believe in the **Who**. And with every breath I have, I will praise the Lord.

"Those who hope in the Lord will renew their strength. They will soar on wings like eagles; they will run and not grow weary, they will walk and not be faint." - Isaiah 40:31

So when life throws curveballs, and it will: stand firm. Keep walking. Keep believing. Because God is not finished with your story. In fact, **your life is about to take a beautiful turn**. Something amazing is coming.

Get ready. He's doing it for His glory, and your good.

Pray with me

Father God,

Thank You for never giving up on me. Thank You for the dream You placed in my heart, even when I've doubted it, even when I've felt alone. Help me trust You when I can't see the way. Remind me that Your timing is perfect. Even when the journey is long, help me believe that Your plan is still unfolding. Give me strength to keep walking, faith to keep believing, and peace to wait on You. Use every part of my story for Your glory. I surrender my plan for Yours.

In Jesus' name,
Amen.

Day 20

Just You and God

Before the year flies by any faster, I want to ask you something real: **something only you can answer**. When was the last time you did something just for you, without asking for permission, without checking with anyone to make sure it was okay, and without feeling guilty? Or maybe the better question is: how close are you to the dream that's been in your heart since before you even knew how to name it?

Have you buried it? Did you give up on it? Or are you still carrying it around, waiting for the right moment?

And if that dream hasn't happened yet, **have you talked to God about it lately?** Not with polished words or a memorized prayer, but in a real, raw conversation? When was the last time you were truly honest with Him? Told Him how you're really doing, what you really want, and where you're truly struggling?

Some of us were raised to think of God as distant, or only there when things fall apart. Others were taught that you have to go through someone else to speak to Him, or that your prayers need to sound holy or perfect.

But God's not looking for a performance. He's after your presence. Your heart. ***"You will seek Me and find Me when you seek Me with all your heart."* - Jeremiah 29:13**

A lot of us are listening to every voice but His. We chase advice. Seek validation. We wait for a sign, a green light, or some kind of confirmation: something we think only someone else can give us. We've grown used to secondhand faith and forgotten we have full access to the Father.

And for some reason, **we still hesitate.**

Maybe someone told you there's a **"right"** way to pray. Maybe they said you shouldn't question God, or that your needs aren't important enough to bring up. Maybe you've stopped praying for yourself altogether. Just waiting for someone else to carry you to Him.

But hear me: you don't need anyone's permission to talk to God. You don't need the perfect words. **You just need to come.**

The Bible says f**ear has to do with punishment**. But God's love is perfect, and perfect love casts out fear. So if fear is running the show, ask yourself: **What are you really afraid of? Who told you that God is disappointed in you? That you're not enough?**

Maybe it's time to wake up; not just physically, but spiritually. To stop shrinking. To stop hiding. To stop waiting for permission to live the life God already called you to.

Right now, I'm sitting here, music playing in the background, reflecting on how real my relationship with God has become. I talk to Him about everything. I love Him, and I know He loves me. I bring Him the good, the messy, and all the stuff in between.

"Blessed is the one whose transgressions are forgiven, whose sins are covered. Blessed is the one whose sin the Lord does not count against them and in whose spirit is no deceit."
- Psalm 32:1-2

My daughter's the same with me: Open, honest, fearless. She doesn't wait for the right moment or try to clean up her words. She just talks to her dad. And I listen.

One time, I told a coworker how my daughter tells me everything, and she said something I'll never forget: **"If your child can't come to you with everything, somewhere along the way, you failed them."**

That stuck with me. And it reminded me, that's how I come to God. I hold nothing back. And He doesn't want you to either. He already knows it all. **He just wants time with you. Time to love on you. To fill you. To remind you of the life He's dreamed for you.** A life better than anything you've imagined.

You don't need a script. You don't need to earn it. You just need to show up.

In **1 Samuel**, when Samuel thought David's older brother would be the next king because of how impressive he looked, God said: *"People look at the outward appearance, but the Lord looks at the heart."*

He's not moved by titles, status, or your latest success. He's moved by your heart. And that's all He wants: you, just as you are.

If you seek Him with your whole heart, He promises you'll find Him. He's not hiding. He's waiting. And He wants something deeper than Sunday routines and surface prayers.

Some of my favorite memories with my daughter are when we're just hanging out, laughing, talking, being ourselves. There's nothing forced, nothing scripted - just presence. That's where our relationship grows. That's where trust is built. That's where love is strengthened.

And every time, I'm reminded, that's what God wants with us.

So stop overthinking it. Stop doubting yourself. Stop believing the lie that you have to clean yourself up before you come. Just come. He already knows you. He already loves you. And He already has a plan for your life that's bigger than what you've been settling for. The question is: **Will you let Him in?**

Pray with me

Father God,

Thank You for loving me: completely, fully, without conditions. Thank You for seeing me, even when I feel invisible. Help me trust You again. Help me talk to You honestly. Show me how to bring every part of myself before You. Remind me that I don't have to be perfect: I just have to be present. Help me let go of fear, shame, guilt, and the lies that keep me distant. Awaken the dream You placed in me. Show me how to walk in it. Thank You for being a Father who listens, who loves, and who never leaves. I give You my heart.

In Jesus' name,
Amen.

Day 21

Which Side Will You Stand On?

I was watching a video this morning: an experiment designed to test the hearts of everyday people. In the clip, a man casually walked up to another and patted him on the back. The unsuspecting man smiled and kept walking, unaware that a degrading image had been taped to his back in that moment.

What followed was telling.

Crowds of people saw it. Some laughed. Some pulled out their phones to record or take pictures. Most just walked by, doing absolutely nothing. No one stopped him. No one spoke up. No one said, **"Hey, there's something on your back."**

And as I sat there watching, something shifted in me, because this wasn't just an experiment. This is real life. We see it every day. In our families. At work. On our phones. We see wrong happening, and still - we stay silent.

But the video didn't end there.

Another group of people passed by, and their response was different. One by one, they removed the image. Some ripped it up. Some crumbled it in their hands. Some told the man what had been done behind his back. They stepped in, not because they had to, **but because it was right**.

And that's the moment that asked me a deeper question: Which side will we stand on? Will we be the ones who stay silent, or the ones who step in?

You don't always have to speak to make a difference: sometimes your presence says more than words ever could. But doing nothing is still a choice. When someone is hurting, check on them. When they're struggling, stand beside them. And when you see something wrong, don't look away.

Jesus said in **John 15:12**, *"This is my commandment, that you love one another as I have loved you."* And in **Galatians 5:14**, *"For the whole law is fulfilled in one word: 'You shall love your neighbor as yourself.'"*

But how can we love our neighbor if we don't know what love really looks like?

Sometimes love is a simple act of kindness. Sometimes it's just listening. And sometimes, it's ripping that image off someone's back, even when no one else will.

I remember a time when I stayed quiet. I saw something wrong and walked away, telling myself it wasn't my business. But God used that moment to teach me something: **what you ignore, you allow. And what you allow, you become a part of.**

Jesus knew betrayal would come. In **John 6:70**, He said, *"Did I not choose you, the Twelve? And yet one of you is a devil."*

Judas walked with Him, prayed with Him, witnessed miracles, and still betrayed Him.

Even Peter, who swore loyalty to Jesus, denied Him three times. But Jesus didn't discard him. In **Luke 22:31-32**, Jesus said, *"Simon, Simon, Satan has asked to sift all of you as wheat. But I have prayed for you... and when you have turned back, strengthen your brothers."*

That means Jesus knew Peter would fall. But He also knew Peter would come back.

Peter went on to preach one of the greatest sermons in **Acts 2**, leading over 3,000 people to salvation. That's the grace of God. **Where you start isn't where you have to finish.**

Some of you reading this are silently carrying a burden no one knows about. You're smiling, but struggling. You're showing up, but you're worn out. And others may not see it, **but God does**.

Some of you have been betrayed by those you trusted most. Others have been overlooked, dismissed, or even laughed at by those who should've lifted you up. And now, in the quiet of your pain, you're asking, **"God... where are You in all of this?"**

Let me remind you: He is close to the brokenhearted and saves those who are crushed in spirit **(Psalm 34:18)**. You are not forgotten. Not by the One who matters most.

And if you've been the one who walked by... the one who stayed silent... the one who laughed...Here's the truth: **It's not too late.** God's mercy is new every morning **(Lamentations 3:22–23)**.

Today, you can choose differently. Choose love. Choose courage. Choose to reflect the heart of Jesus. Ask God for **discernment**, because not everyone in your life is sent by God, and not every enemy is meant for harm. **Sometimes your greatest breakthroughs come from the most unexpected places.**

And above all: **walk in love**. Jesus didn't just lay His life down for you. He did it for the world. He did it for the ones who hurt Him, denied Him, and mocked Him. That's the love we're called to reflect.

Because sometimes, the smallest act of love carries the loudest echo in someone's life.

Pray with me

Father God,

Father God, thank You for opening my eyes. Forgive me for the times I stayed silent, for the moments I turned away instead of leaning in. Give me courage to stand for what's right, even when it's uncomfortable. Give me discernment to know who is for me and who is not. Teach me to love like You: with compassion, truth, and boldness. And if I've fallen short, remind me that You're not done with me. You're the God of redemption. Make my heart more like Yours, and help me be a light in someone else's darkness.

In Jesus' name,
Amen.

Day 22

What Are You Running From?

You feel it, don't you? There's something moving deep inside you, something pressing against your heart so intensely that you can no longer ignore it. It keeps you up at night, tossing and turning, your mind racing with thoughts you can't seem to shake. You try to push them aside, distract yourself, pretend they're not there, **but they are**. And they won't go away. This isn't just a passing thought or feeling. It's God calling you, whispering, **"It's time."**

But here's the question: **are you feeding your fear and starving your faith?**

If you find yourself hesitating, maybe it's time to stop running. *"Be still, and know that I am God"* (Psalm 46:10). No matter how far you go, no matter how much you try to blend into the crowd, **you can never hide from God**. And why would you want to? He's the One who formed you, the One who knows you better than you know yourself. That calling that won't let go of you? He placed it inside of you before you ever took your first breath.

I know what it's like to wake up in the middle of the night, frustrated because morning is coming too fast. But what if those restless nights aren't just sleepless moments? **What if they're divine wake-up calls?** What if the discomfort you keep brushing off is God's way of trying to get your attention?

You see the **signs everywhere**: a conversation, on TV, social media, a sermon, even moments of silence that feel heavy with meaning. And yet, you keep ignoring them. So God does what He does best: **He isolates you.** He removes distractions, silences the noise, and makes sure that His voice is the only one you can hear. He did it with Paul on the Damascus Road. He did it with Moses in the wilderness. He did it with Joseph in the pit. And now, **He's doing it with you.**

It's okay to feel afraid. Even Ezekiel struggled with his calling **(Ezekiel 3:14-15)**. But his hesitation didn't change the fact that he was chosen. **And neither does yours.**

You are **called** to something greater, and it's not for your glory; it's for God's. Don't abort the mission. Some of you are at the end of your wilderness season, standing on the edge of your promised land. But don't let doubt and disobedience delay your breakthrough.

The Israelites journey to the promise land should have taken **eleven days**. Instead, it took **forty years**. Not because of the enemy, but because they doubted, complained, and refused to trust the God who had already proven Himself. How many years have you lost because of fear?

"Faith the size of a mustard seed" can move mountains **(Matthew 17:20)**. Don't let fear prolong your journey. There is a shift happening right now. God is positioning His people for greatness. This is not the time to hesitate. This is the time to step forward in faith. ***"Be strong and courageous. Do not be afraid; do not be discouraged, for the Lord your God will be with you wherever you go"* (Joshua 1:9).** When God calls you, He equips you. When He sends you, He goes with you. **You are never alone.**

I remember the loneliest time in my life; when I first confessed that Jesus was Lord. But looking back, I realize I wasn't alone; I was being prepared. **Maybe you're waiting on God's perfect timing, but what if He's waiting on you?** Sometimes He isolates you to make His voice clearer, to quiet the chaos in your mind. Some of us have allowed too many voices to drown out His. If you're struggling to hear Him, maybe it's time to remove the distractions.

The time is now. If you were waiting for a sign, **here it is**. When your **"yes"** is real, your life will never look the same. **The people around you won't look the same; not because they've changed, but because you have.** You have shifted. You have surrendered. And now, you have nowhere left to run.
`

Lift your hands. Surrender. God is calling. **It's faith over fear.**

Pray with me

Heavenly Father,

I hear You. I feel You moving in my life, calling me to step forward in faith. No more running. No more excuses. I surrender. Lead me, guide me, and give me the strength to walk boldly in the purpose You have for me. I choose faith over fear. I trust You completely.

In Jesus' name,
Amen.

Day 23

Who Do You Say You Are?

I was watching a movie one day when one of the actors asked a question that stuck with me: **"When it's all said and done, what do you want to be most remembered for?"**

The other actor paused, rubbing his chin, eyes filled with curiosity. **"You know, no one has ever asked me that question,"** he said. After a moment of thought, he laughed. **"I really don't know."**

For a long time, I didn't know either. But now? Now I can answer that with confidence. I want to be known for giving my best, for using the gifts God has given me to help as many people as possible. I want to be remembered as someone who wasn't afraid to stand firm in faith, even if that meant standing alone.

One of my favorite quotes says, **"Be bold. Be brave enough to be your true self."**

Authenticity takes courage. It means standing strong in your convictions, even when the world pushes back. Being bold is stepping out in faith when the path is uncertain. Being brave is trusting God when He calls you beyond your comfort zone.

Being true to yourself isn't about following your heart, it's about aligning your life with the purpose God designed for you.

Before God called me out of the darkness, I had no direction, no purpose, and no identity. **I was lost**, searching for answers to questions I didn't even know how to ask. I was just going through life, unsure of who I was or where I was headed.

Then, one day at Ashmont Station in Boston, a man I had run into before approached me. Each time, he would invite me to church, and each time, my answer was the same: **"Don't be surprised if you see me there one day."** But I never showed up.

This time was different. He didn't just invite me: he challenged me.

"When are you going to take your relationship with God seriously?" he asked. I just looked at him and smiled. Then he asked if I'd be interested in studying the Bible with him and some of the guys from his church. Again, I hesitated.

"I don't even have a Bible," I finally admitted.

What he did next changed my life forever. He unzipped his backpack, pulled out a small, used Bible, and handed it to me.

"Now you do," he said.

It was as if, in that moment, **my entire life shifted**. I knew God was calling me. I could feel it. That was the day everything changed. **Jeremiah 29:13** says, *"You will seek me and find me when you seek me with all your heart."* That day, I wasn't even seeking Him, **but He found me anyway**.

Jesus lived with boldness, bravery, and authenticity. He knew His journey would not be easy, yet He trusted the Father completely. He spent time with Him, leaned on Him, and drew strength from Him.

In **Matthew 16**, after His followers returned to Him, Jesus asked two questions: **"Who do the people say I am?"**

They responded with various answers. But it was His second question that truly mattered: **"Who do you say I am?"**

Only Peter answered correctly, declaring, **"You are the Messiah, the Son of the living God."**

That moment was powerful. Peter recognized Jesus for who He truly was.

Now, let me ask you: **Who do people say you are?** Your family, your friends, your coworkers: what do they see in you? Do they see someone who reflects Jesus, or someone who blends into the world?

More importantly, **who does Jesus say you are?**

This is where self-discovery meets faith. It's not just about understanding yourself, it's about understanding yourself through God's eyes. We all struggle with identity at some point. The world tries to define us by achievements, status, appearance, or past mistakes. But those things don't define you: **God does**.

When Jesus said, *"I am the true vine"* (**John 15:1**), He was giving us a clear message: apart from Him, **we can do nothing**. He is our source of strength, wisdom, and purpose. Imagine a vine. The branches don't bear fruit on their own: they only thrive when connected to the vine. That's **us and Jesus**.

If we asked God, **"Who do You say I am?"** we would want Him to say: **"You are My child. You are chosen, set apart, created for a purpose. You are strong in Me. You are called to bring light into the darkness, to love without condition, to stand boldly in truth. You are Mine."**

That's the identity we should be striving for, not one shaped by this world, but one shaped by God's truth. Faith isn't about having all the answers: **none of us have arrived**. But God isn't asking for perfection; **He's asking for surrender.**

When we trust Him completely, we step into the identity He has given us. We stop chasing approval from the world because His approval is all we need. **Stop waiting for life to change on its own: it won't**. Prayer without action is like planting without watering. If you're believing for something, step into it and move in faith.

The seed God planted in you wasn't meant to stay buried. It's been nurtured and is ready to break through. Don't let fear or the opinions of others stop you from stepping into your calling. What God placed in you is meant to grow and bear fruit.

The gifts He's given you are waiting to be unlocked, but they won't open themselves. It's time. Trust Him, step forward, and watch what He does.

Pray with me

Heavenly Father,

Thank You for creating me with purpose. Help me to see myself through Your eyes, not the world's. Strengthen me to be bold in faith, brave in obedience, and true to who You've called me to be. I surrender my doubts, my fears, and my need for approval. I want to live fully for You, walking in confidence, knowing that I am Yours.

In Jesus' name,
Amen.

Day 24

Who Told You That You Couldn't?

Do you realize the power that's inside of you? Not just the kind of power that helps you get through the day, but the kind of power that **breaks barriers, erase limits, and changes your life**.

The truth is, you can do anything you set your mind to. Yes, anything. That dream you've been holding onto? That goal you've been afraid to chase? It's within reach. But somewhere along the way, someone convinced you that you couldn't. Maybe it was a person's words. Maybe it was years of doubt. Maybe it was fear whispering in your ear, planting the thought that you are not enough. And now, you're stuck believing a lie.

The mind is powerful. Whatever you feed it will grow. What you listen to, what you accept, what you allow to take root in your spirit: it all shapes the way you see yourself, the way you think, and ultimately, the way you live. **Proverbs 18:21** reminds us. *"The tongue has the power of life and death."*

Some people have talked themselves out of greatness without even realizing it. Some have let the wrong voices shape their identity. Some have believed lies that were never true in the first place.

So let me ask you: c**an you recognize the truth from a lie?**

Think about Adam and Eve. Before they ate the forbidden fruit, they had everything—paradise, perfect peace, unlimited access to God. They lacked nothing. But one wrong voice changed everything.

Genesis 3:1 says, *"Now the serpent was more cunning than any beast of the field which the Lord God had made."* The serpent didn't force Eve to eat the fruit. He didn't have to. All he did was plant doubt.

"Did God really say…?"

That one question was enough to shift her entire perspective. One seed of uncertainty, one twisted version of the truth, and suddenly, she saw what was off-limits as something desirable. And isn't that exactly how the enemy still works today? He doesn't always come at you with something obvious. He waits. He watches. He studies you.

Then, when you're tired, vulnerable, or alone, he whispers. **"You'll never be good enough. God doesn't really care about you. You're too broken to be used. You'll always be stuck."** And if you hear those lies enough times, you start to believe them.

1 John 4:1 warns us to *"test the spirits to see whether they are from God, because many false prophets have gone out into the world."* This is a reminder to be discerning in who you listen to. Not every voice is from God.

The enemy's goal has always been the same: to steal, kill, and destroy. But his first attack isn't on your finances, your relationships, or your health. He starts with your mind. Because if he can get you to believe the wrong things about yourself, about God, and about your purpose, then he doesn't need to do anything else. You'll defeat yourself.

But here's the good news: **Jesus came to set you free.**

You don't have to live trapped in fear, doubt, or insecurity. The truth will set you free. **John 8:32** tells us, *"Then you will know the truth, and the truth will set you free."* Jesus is the truth, and through Him, we find freedom from every lie that holds us back.

That's why discernment is so important. Not every voice in your life is from God. Not every word spoken over you is meant for you. Be careful who you allow to pour into you. Even the believers in the Bible didn't just take Paul's word for things: they checked the Scriptures daily to make sure what he said was true **(Acts 17:11)**.

So I ask you again: **who has been speaking into your life? Who told you that you couldn't? Who convinced you that you weren't enough?** Because it wasn't God.

It's time to break free. You are not stuck. You are not defeated. You are not disqualified. The life you've been longing for isn't some far-off dream. If you want a better life, you can have it. If you want financial freedom, you can build it. If you want peace, joy, and purpose, you can step into it. But you have to make a choice.

The battle isn't against people, it's a spiritual fight. The enemy wants to keep you distracted, discouraged, and defeated. But God says you are more than a conqueror. He says you are chosen, loved, and called for something greater. And yet, the enemy will do everything in his power to keep you from believing that.

So here's the truth: you have **two choices**. You can believe what God says about you, or you can believe the lies of the enemy. You can choose faith, or you can choose fear. You can step into your calling, or you can stay stuck in self-doubt. But you cannot do both. **It's time to decide.**

Pray with me

God,

Thank You for the power You've placed inside of me. Help me to see the truth of who I am in You. Guide me to trust in Your promises and remember that with You, all things are possible. Show me how to ignore the lies and focus on the truth of Your Word. Give me strength to break free from anything holding me back and courage to step into the life You've called me to live. Thank You for Your love, grace, and the power to overcome.

In Jesus' name,
Amen.

Day 25

Destiny Helper or Destiny Thief?

A few days ago, I came across a video that stopped me in my tracks. A kid was opening a box of sneakers he had clearly wanted, but what stood out wasn't just his excitement. It was the reaction of the friend or younger brother beside him. The moment he saw what was inside, his whole face lit up. He gave him a high-five and started celebrating like he had just received the shoes himself.

That moment was about more than sneakers. It was a pure, unfiltered display of joy for someone else's blessing. No jealousy. No **"I wish it were me."** Just genuine happiness for someone else's win.

And it made me ask: **Are you a Destiny Helper or a Destiny Thief?**

A **Destiny Helper** is someone who encourages, supports, and uplifts others. They push you closer to your purpose, helping you grow into the person you were meant to be. These are the people who celebrate your victories and stand by you through challenges. They cheer you on, even when they're still waiting for their own breakthrough.

A **Destiny Thief**, on the other hand, does the opposite. Some do it intentionally: spreading negativity, discouraging your dreams, or secretly hoping you fail. Others don't even realize they're doing it, but they drain your energy, plant seeds of doubt, or lead you away from your purpose. They make you question your own abilities, distract you with unnecessary drama, or compete with you when they should be supporting you.

One of the earliest examples of a Destiny Thief is found in the story of Cain and Abel. Both brothers made offerings to God, but Abel's was accepted while Cain's was not. Instead of learning from it, improving, or celebrating his brother's favor, Cain allowed jealousy to consume him. He let bitterness take root, and it led him to do the unthinkable: take his own brother's life.

God had warned him, saying, *"If you do what is right, will you not be accepted? But if you do not do what is right, sin is crouching at your door; it desires to have you, but you must rule over it."* (Genesis 4:7)

Cain didn't listen. He let his emotions turn him into a Destiny Thief, robbing his brother of his future and himself of God's blessing.

Now, ask yourself: **Are you your brother's keeper, or does someone else's success make you feel like you're falling behind? Do you celebrate others, or does their progress make you uncomfortable?**

Even Jesus wasn't exempt from Destiny Thieves. He had one walking beside Him: Judas. **This was a man who had seen Jesus perform miracles, walked with Him, eaten with Him, and yet, for thirty pieces of silver, he betrayed the One who came to save him.**

Judas wasn't just a Destiny Thief to Jesus: he was one to himself. Instead of repenting, he let his guilt consume him. And that's the thing about being a Destiny Thief: it doesn't just hurt the other person. It hurts you too.

But Jesus? He was the ultimate Destiny Helper. He lifted people up, healing the sick, encouraging the brokenhearted, and restoring the outcasts. He sacrificed for others, laying down His life so we could live in freedom. He believed in people: even the ones the world had given up on. Jesus didn't compete, He completed.

So ask yourself honestly: **Are you helping or hurting?**

When your friend gets a promotion, do you celebrate or secretly feel like it should have been you? When someone shares their dream with you, do you encourage them or plant doubt? When people around you win, do you clap for them or compare?

God has a plan for everyone. There's room for all of us at the table. You don't need to take from someone else to receive what God has for you.

The Bible reminds us, *"I can do all things through Christ who strengthens me."* **(Philippians 4:13)**

God didn't make a mistake when He created you. You are uniquely designed for a purpose. Instead of envying someone else's path, focus on walking your own.

Will you be a **Destiny Helper**, encouraging and uplifting others? Or a **Destiny Thief**, allowing jealousy and negativity to rob both you and others of God's plan? **Choose wisely**.

Pray with me

Heavenly Father,

Thank You for the life and purpose You have given me. Forgive me for any jealousy, comparison, or negativity I've allowed into my heart. Help me to be a Destiny Helper, someone who lifts others up, spreads love, and brings glory to You. Keep me from being a Destiny Thief, and remind me that my journey is mine alone. Let me walk in purpose, with confidence, knowing that what You have for me is for me.

In Jesus' name,
Amen.

Day 26

You Are Enough

If you're in the habit of comparing yourself to others or measuring your worth by what someone else has or does, I'm here to tell you: **stop**.

The problem with comparison is that it makes what you have seem less valuable. When you measure your life against someone else's, you stop seeing yourself through God's eyes. You start believing you're falling short because, by their standards, you're not where you "should" be.

It's like ordering a steak dinner, perfectly cooked, with all your favorite sides. But then you see the table next to you, where someone else is eating salmon, and suddenly, your meal doesn't seem as good. Nothing about your meal changed—only your perspective. The same thing happens when you compare your car, your job, or even your calling to someone else's. You begin to believe what they have is better, and what God gave you isn't enough.

But who told you that? Certainly not God.

I remember trying out for my high school basketball team. The moment I stepped into the gym, I scanned the room, sizing up every other point guard. I watched their every move: who was faster, who could jump higher, who had better ball-handling skills. In my mind, I had already disqualified myself. I wasn't measuring my potential; I was measuring my shortcomings. I focused so much on what I **couldn't** do that I forgot about the skills I **did** have. It wasn't until I shifted my mindset: until I stopped comparing and started trusting in the abilities God had given me, that everything changed. Not only did I make the team, but I became a starter.

And isn't that what we do in life? We waste time focusing on what others are doing instead of using what God has given us.

The world is full of copycats: people trying to look, act, and live like someone else. Imitation may be a form of flattery, but God didn't create you to be a replica. He created you to be you. There's only one you, and that's exactly how God intended it.

Spiritually, this same issue exists. Some people chase after preachers, influencers, or leaders instead of seeking after God. Paul addressed this when he said,

"One of you says, 'I follow Paul'; another, 'I follow Apollos'; another, 'I follow Cephas.' Is Christ divided? Was Paul crucified for you?" (1 Corinthians 1:12-13)

Far too often, we align ourselves with human leaders instead of with Jesus. But our calling isn't to follow people: **it's to follow Him.**

Look at David. When Saul tried to give him his armor before facing Goliath, it didn't fit. Why? Because it wasn't what God had equipped him with. Instead, David used what he had: his slingshot, his skill, and his faith. And that's all he needed.

Some of us are trying to wear someone else's armor. We're forcing ourselves into a role, a lifestyle, or a calling that was never meant for us. But God doesn't want you to be like someone else. He wants you to be like Jesus.

1 Corinthians 12:4-6 reminds us, *"There are different kinds of gifts, but the same Spirit distributes them. There are different kinds of service, but the same Lord. There are different kinds of working, but in all of them and in everyone, it is the same God at work."*

God has placed something in you that no one else can carry out in the way He intended.

If you're waiting for permission to step into what God has called you to do: here it is.

If you feel led to write a book, start writing.
If you feel called to start a business, take the first step.
If you want to be a teacher, a lawyer, a speaker: go after it.

Stop letting comparison hold you back. Everything you need, God has already put inside of you. He formed you with purpose, on purpose. **Jeremiah 1:5** says, *"Before I formed you in the womb I knew you, before you were born I set you apart."*

With God, you can do and be all things. Step into who He created you to be. Start today.

Pray with me

Heavenly Father,

Thank You for creating me with purpose. Forgive me for the times I've compared myself to others and doubted what You've placed inside of me. Help me to see myself the way You see me: chosen, loved, and equipped for the calling You've placed on my life. Give me the courage to walk in confidence, to embrace my gifts, and to trust that I am enough because You are enough. May my life bring You glory in all things.

**In Jesus' name,
Amen.**

Day 27

Be the Change Someone Needs

I remember watching an older episode of *The Oprah Winfrey Show* where a young woman was struggling with anorexia. She weighed just 58 pounds, but it wasn't just her frail body that caught my attention: it was the look in her eyes. A silent cry for help.

Onstage with her was another woman who had overcome the disease. She spoke with hope, trying to encourage her: **"You can get through this."** But you could see the pain in the young woman's eyes. She wasn't convinced. She responded with the only words she could find: **"But how?"**

That moment stayed with me.

How often do we tell people what to do: what path to take, what choice to make, without walking with them through it? Advice is easy to give, but for someone lost in their struggle, sometimes words aren't enough. Sometimes, they don't need a blueprint: they need a guide.

Jesus understood this.

He didn't just tell people about God's love, He showed them. He walked with the disciples, built relationships, and taught with compassion. He healed the broken, fed the hungry, and wept with those who mourned. And in the greatest act of love, He gave His life on the cross: not just to tell us the way, but to **be** the way.

"This is how we know what love is: Jesus Christ laid down His life for us. And we ought to lay down our lives for our brothers and sisters." **(1 John 3:16)**

I think back to when I first started working out. I walked into the gym, unsure of what to do. I fumbled with the weights, trying to figure it out on my own. Then a guy came over and said, **"You're going to hurt yourself lifting that way."**

At first, I wanted to tell him to mind his own business. But instead, I asked, **"What am I doing wrong?"**

Instead of just telling me, he showed me. He corrected my form, introduced me to others, and soon, I was training with them 4 to 5 days a week. Over time, I got stronger. I gained confidence. And eventually, I found myself teaching others, because someone took the time to walk with me, not just talk at me.

The same is true for our faith.

People don't just need to hear about God's love: they need to see it.

"Let us not love with words or speech but with actions and in truth." **(1 John 3:18)**

Think about that young woman on *Oprah*. When she asked **"How?"** She wasn't asking for more words. She was asking for someone to **be her how**.

When was the last time you became someone's **how**? When was the last time you showed up for someone God assigned to you?

Jesus showed up when we couldn't show up for ourselves. He was our how when we felt lost and abandoned. Now, He calls us to do the same for others.

Galatians 6:2 says, *"Carry each other's burdens, and in this way you will fulfill the law of Christ."*

God doesn't just want us to tell people about Him: He wants us to **demonstrate** His love. Sometimes, the **how** is the very thing God will use to bless others and change lives. When you take the time to invest in someone, you become the hands and feet of Jesus in their life.

1 John 3:18 reminds us, *"Dear children, let us not love with words or speech but with actions and in truth."*

Maybe your **how** is offering a listening ear to someone who is struggling. Maybe it's mentoring a younger believer in their faith. Maybe it's forgiving someone who doesn't deserve it, simply because Jesus forgave you.

Whatever it is, don't miss the opportunity to **be the how** for someone who needs it.

When you let go, God moves. When you step out, God steps in. When you **become the how**, God gets the glory.

Pray with me

Heavenly Father,

Thank You for being my how when I couldn't find my way. Thank You for showing me grace, love, and truth through Your Son, Jesus. Help me to live out my faith: not just in words but in action. Show me the people You've assigned to me, and give me the courage to walk with them. May my life bring You glory in all things.

In Jesus' name,
Amen.

Day 28

When You Let Go, God Moves

What If Your Life Was a Movie?

Have you ever watched a show, game, or movie and found yourself yelling at the screen, frustrated by what's happening? You act like the characters can hear you, but they can't.

Now, imagine someone secretly recorded the last two weeks of your life. Picture your family, friends, coworkers, and loved ones gathered in a theater, about to watch it all unfold on the big screen.

As the movie begins, you realize: **you are the main character.**

Would you watch with confidence, or would there be moments you wish you could erase? Would you feel embarrassed by the way you acted, the things you said, or the choices you made?

That's a tough thought, isn't it?

But here's the reality: God sees it all. ***Nothing in creation is hidden from Him*** (Hebrews 4:13). Yet, we often spend more time worrying about **what people think** rather than **what God knows**.

We try to hide our flaws, struggles, and sins from people, fearing judgment. But the truth is, **God is the only one whose approval truly matters.**

Many of us are carrying things we were never meant to hold onto **unforgiveness, anger, bitterness, and shame**.

Just because someone is saved or appears to have it all together **doesn't mean they aren't struggling with something deep inside**. Some people feel trapped, afraid to let anyone see the real them, fearing rejection.

But here's the thing: **God already knows, and He still loves you**.

Jeremiah 17:5 warns us: *"Cursed is the person who trusts in man and makes flesh his strength, whose heart turns away from the Lord."*

Depending on people alone for validation, healing, or acceptance will always leave us empty. **Only God can fill that void**.

One of the hardest things in life; whether you're a believer or not, is **forgiving** yourself or someone who has hurt you.

I'll never forget what someone told me when I first gave my life to Christ. "The people in the church will hurt you more than the people in the world."

I laughed it off, until months later when those very words became my reality. The hurt was real, and I almost walked away from the church completely.

But then I remembered Jesus' words in **Matthew 18:21-22**: *"Lord, how many times should I forgive my brother or sister who sins against me? Seven times?" Jesus replied, "Not seven times, but seventy-seven times."*

Jesus was saying, **forgiveness isn't about keeping score, it's about setting yourself free.**

Holding onto bitterness keeps you trapped in the pain. But when you release it to God, you're set free.

People will let you down. Promises will be broken. Some people will hurt you: **intentionally or unintentionally**. And often, it's those closest to us.

But here's a question to consider: **How many times have we hurt God?** Yet, despite our failures, He loves us unconditionally. Despite our mistakes, He forgives us completely.

The Bible says, *"How can you say you love God if you hate your brother or sister?"* (1 John 4:20).

Jesus commands us, *"Love one another so that people will know you are my disciples."* (John 13:34-35)

Forgiveness doesn't mean forgetting, it means trusting God with the outcome. It means letting go so you can move forward.

Want to see a miracle? Go look in the mirror. Yes, **YOU** are a miracle. The fact that you are alive today, reading this message, means God still has a purpose for you.

You want to see love? **Read the Bible**.
You want to experience freedom? S**urrender to God**.

When Jesus was in the Garden of Gethsemane, knowing He was about to be betrayed, beaten, and crucified, He still prayed: *"Father, if You are willing, take this cup from Me. Yet not My will, but Yours be done."* (Luke 22:42)

He knew the suffering ahead, yet He chose obedience. **He chose the cross because He chose YOU**.

And in His final moments, hanging between two criminals, He uttered the most powerful words: *"Father, forgive them, for they know not what they do."* (Luke 23:34)

If Jesus could forgive the very people who nailed Him to the cross, what is stopping us from forgiving others?

Your destiny is ahead of you, not behind you. Your breakthrough is in front of you. God has already given you the strength to overcome - **He's just waiting for you to take the step. When you let go, God will move.**

Pray with me

Lord,

Thank You for seeing me, knowing me, and loving me despite my flaws. I surrender my burdens, my pain, and my unforgiveness to You. Help me to walk in freedom and extend the same grace You've given me to others. Strengthen me to trust You fully and live for Your glory.

In Jesus' name,
Amen.

Day 29

The Power of Being Alone With God

Some people think being alone is a problem. But being alone isn't about loneliness, it's about growth. It's about stepping away from the noise of the world so you can hear God's voice more clearly. In **silence, He gives you direction. In stillness, He gives you strength.**

When you make time to be alone with God, you give Him room to **speak into your life**. He shows you who you are, what He's called you to do, and where He's leading you. Without distractions, you begin to see what truly matters. **You begin to hear His voice above all others**.

Even Jesus stepped away from the crowds to be alone with the Father. **Luke 5:16** says, *"But Jesus often withdrew to lonely places and prayed."* If the Son of God needed time alone to stay strong and focused, how much more do we?

Solitude isn't about shutting people out; it's about **making space for God**. In those quiet moments, He refreshes your spirit, renews your mind, and prepares you for what's ahead.

For me, time alone with God is like hitting the reset button: a chance for Him to shape my heart, clear my mind, and remind me that His plan is greater than mine. When I was writing *The Hidden Exchange*, I spent hours in quiet, just me, my thoughts, and **God's undeniable presence**. In that stillness, He showed me things I never would have seen on my own. My purpose became clearer, and I poured my heart into the work He had placed in my hands.

Some of the best decisions you will ever make will happen when you are alone with God. My daughter has been journaling since November 2023, and since January 2025, she hasn't missed a single day. When I asked her why, she said, **"Journaling helps me understand my thoughts and express my feelings."** That's what writing does for me, too. Though I don't journal like her, I find peace in putting words on paper. Writing is where I meet God, hear from Him, and feel closest to Him.

Maybe for you, solitude looks different. Maybe it's going for a walk, spending time in prayer, reading scripture, or sitting in silence with no distractions. However it happens, one thing is certain: God meets you in the quiet.

The world will always demand your attention. The texts will keep coming. The responsibilities will always be there. But you cannot pour from an empty cup. Even Jesus took time to rest. **Mark 6:31** says, *"Come with me by yourselves to a quiet place and get some rest."*

So don't feel guilty for **stepping away** when you need to refuel. Don't feel bad for saying no when your soul is weary. **Take time to sit with God, to listen, to process, and to just be. Your spirit needs it. Your purpose requires it.**

The next time you find yourself alone, don't see it as isolation, see it as an invitation. God is calling you deeper. He wants to reveal things to you that you **can't hear in the noise of every-day life. Accept His invitation**.

Pray with me

Heavenly Father,

Thank You for the gift of solitude. Thank You for meeting me in the quiet moments and revealing Your heart to me. Help me to see alone time not as loneliness, but as an opportunity to grow closer to You. Give me wisdom to step away when I need to refuel and the discernment to hear Your voice above all others. Strengthen me, guide me, and fill me with Your peace.

In Jesus' name,
Amen.

Day 30

You Were Made for This

I remember my first day of college as one of the happiest moments of my life. But when my family loaded the car and drove away, reality hit me like a wave. What had possessed me to choose a school so far from home, away from everything and everyone familiar? Before stepping foot on campus, I thought I had made the right decision: until I was alone, surrounded by strangers, wondering where I fit in.

After a few days, the excitement wore off, and the loneliness set in. I picked up the phone and called my mother. "I need to come home," I told her. "I'm homesick." But the truth was, I was craving the comfort of the familiar. She listened patiently for a minute before she interrupted me.

"We will always be here for you, but this next journey in your life is yours to figure out. It won't be easy. You'll face challenges, and some will test you. But you will get through them. God has prepared you for this moment, and you are so much stronger than you realize." Then she finished with words I'll never forget: "I'm so proud of the man you are becoming." And before I could respond, she hung up.

As I walked back to my dorm room, I didn't say, I can't let my family down. I can't let my friends down. No. I said, **I can't let myself down**. I hadn't even given myself a chance, and yet, I was ready to run. But it was my choice to be here, and my responsibility to see it through. So I stayed. And it was one of the best decisions of my life.

Maybe for you, it's not college. Maybe you're wrestling with the decision to start that business, to go back to school, or to finally walk away from a job that no longer serves you. Maybe you feel stuck, paralyzed by fear, waiting for a sign, a voice, or someone to tell you that you're making the right choice. But your destiny isn't up for debate. It's between you and God.

Sometimes, we want people to hold our hands through the hard times, and there's nothing wrong with that. But in life, you will have to make some tough decisions on your own. Not everyone will understand. Not everyone will agree. Some will call you foolish. Others will say you're making a mistake. But your destiny isn't up for debate. It's between you and God.

Stop overthinking. Stop waiting for outside validation. Sometimes, the answer is already in front of you, but you're too busy seeking approval to see it. Fear will keep you frozen, but God is calling you forward.

God never promised the journey would be easy, but He did promise He would never leave you. *"Be strong and courageous. Do not be afraid or terrified because of them, for the Lord your God goes with you; He will never leave you nor forsake you"* (**Deuteronomy 31:6).** So while you wait, prepare. And where does preparation start? In the mind.

How many times have you shared your vision with someone, only for them to talk you out of it? You go to another person, hoping for a different response, but they discourage you too. Before you know it, you're right back where you started; doubting yourself, stuck in fear, further from the path God set for you.

Your mistake? You sought people's approval before seeking God's direction. ***"Commit to the Lord whatever you do, and He will establish your plans"*** **(Proverbs 16:3)**.

There will always be people who say you can't or won't. Not because you aren't capable, but because they're afraid you will. They didn't take the leap, so they don't want you to either. But their fear is not your future.

Stop waiting for people to affirm what God already confirmed. The only approval you need is His. And when you trust Him, He will align the right people in your life: people who will celebrate your greatness and push you toward your purpose.

Paul said in **Galatians 1:10**, *"If I were still trying to please people, I would not be a servant of Christ."*

I think back to my mother's words. In that moment, her advice didn't erase my fear, but it did something far greater. It awakened something inside me. It reminded me that I wasn't just some lost, uncertain young man trying to find his way: **I was called. I was equipped.** And I wasn't walking this path alone.

God had already gone before me. He had already prepared the way. But I had to believe that for myself. My mother saw something in me that I had yet to see in myself. She spoke life into me, silencing the doubts before they had the chance to take root. And in that moment, I made a decision. Not just to stay, but to stand on my faith, on my calling, and on the promise that God had placed inside of me.

And that's what He is saying to you right now. You may feel uncertain. You may feel afraid. But God has already gone ahead of you. He has already equipped you. And now, it's time for you to believe it. To step into it. To rise up and walk in the confidence that He has called you for something greater.

Pray with me

Heavenly Father,

Thank You for preparing me for this moment. Thank You for never leaving me, even when I've doubted myself. Today, I choose to trust You. I release fear, doubt, and the need for approval. I walk in faith, knowing that You have already equipped me for the road ahead. Strengthen me, guide me, and help me to see myself the way You see me.

**In Jesus' name,
Amen.**

Day 31

What Are You Believing God For?

What have you been praying for tirelessly, yet it still hasn't come to pass?

Maybe it's a new job, a fresh start. Maybe it's the courage to walk away from a toxic relationship or a job that has drained every ounce of joy from you. Maybe you're overwhelmed by life, feeling like there's no way out.

Or maybe you're carrying something no one else knows about, a silent struggle, a prayer whispered in the dark: waiting, hoping, but feeling abandoned. Maybe you're exhausted, pouring into everyone else while feeling unseen, unheard, invisible to those closest to you.

But hear me: **God sees you. He has heard your prayers. He is answering-even now.**

Sometimes, the problem isn't that God hasn't answered: it's that we're looking for the answer in the wrong way. God's perspective isn't ours. His ways are higher. What if the door you've been knocking on isn't the one He's opening? What if the enemy has been whispering lies, convincing you that God has left you, when in reality, He's right beside you, waiting for you to shift your focus?

One of the enemy's greatest tactics is to make you believe God has abandoned you. That's a lie straight from the pit of hell. God has promised, *"I will never to leave you or forsake you"* **(Deuteronomy 31:6)**.

You are not alone.

Depression is not your identity.
Worry is not your inheritance.
Fear is not your future.

Maybe you're waiting for a phone call, but God is waiting for you to answer His call. Maybe you don't know what tomorrow holds, but **God never asked you to**. His Word says, *"Do not worry about tomorrow, for tomorrow will worry about itself."* **(Matthew 6:34)** He wants you to live in today.

Instead of chasing people, positions, or possessions: **God wants you to chase Him**.

If God is in the passenger seat of your life, it's time to move over and let Him drive. You don't have to have it all figured out. If you're tired of the uphill battle, weary from feeling stuck, and exhausted from doing it on your own: **surrender.** Submit your will for His. His way is always better.

Many of us carry wounds: unforgiveness, regret, disappointment. We say we're waiting on God, but sometimes, **He's waiting on us to take a step of faith.**

The Bible says, *"**Ask, and you will receive; seek, and you will find; knock, and the door will be opened to you**"* (Matthew 7:7). But faith is key: when you ask, **believe**. When you knock, **be ready to walk through the door**.

God has opened a **new door** for you, but you can't step into what He has prepared until you're willing to **close the old one**.

Let it go. Release it. **What's waiting on the other side of your obedience is greater than anything you're afraid to lose.**

You are not reading this by accident. God is speaking to you, trying to get your attention. **He has been calling, but have you been listening?**

Maybe you've been waiting for a sign. **This is your sign.** It's time to stop letting fear, doubt, and distractions keep you from fully surrendering to Him.

Instead of worrying, seek Him. The Bible says, *"**You will find me when you seek me with all your heart**"* (Jeremiah 29:13). He knows your needs before you even ask. He loves you more than anyone ever could.

If you've been running on empty, now is the time to refuel your soul in His presence. Lay everything at His feet.

Step forward in faith: let go of what's holding you back and walk through the door God has opened for you!

Pray with me

Heavenly Father,

Thank You for seeing me, for loving me, and for never leaving me. I surrender my worries, my fears, and my plans to You. Open my eyes to see what You have already answered. Give me the strength to walk away from anything that pulls me away from You.

Help me to trust You fully, to seek You above all else, and to walk through the doors You have opened for me. I cast my burdens on You, knowing You care for me. Fill me with Your peace, and remind me that I am never alone.

In Jesus' name,
Amen.

Day 32

Are Your Choices Pulling You Closer to God, Or Further Away?

This isn't an easy question: but it's an important one.

Think about the choices you've made recently. Have they drawn you closer to God or taken you further from Him?

We've all made decisions we regret. Maybe you bought something you thought you needed, only to feel that sting of regret later: buyer's remorse. There's a reason for that. **Caveat emptor**: *"let the buyer beware."* Once the purchase is made, the responsibility falls on you.

Life works the same way. Every choice comes with a consequence, whether we like it or not. And at the end of the day, we are exactly where our decisions have led us.

Years ago, I was invited to speak at a church youth event. When I walked in, I could feel the skepticism in the room: curious stares, whispers. I wasn't dressed like the other speakers. No suit. No tie. Just jeans, a polo shirt, and Timberland boots. I knew if I wanted them to listen, I had to meet them where they were.

Ten minutes in, the atmosphere shifted. They leaned in, listening intently as I spoke about choices, the way our desire to fit in can push us down roads we never intended to walk. I shared my own mistakes, the dark places they led me, and how I didn't always make it out unscathed.

When I finished, the usual handshakes and thank-yous followed. But then, three teens approached me.

One young woman, maybe seventeen, locked eyes with me and said, **"You're not like the others. They preach at us. You actually listened."**

I smiled, nodded. But her next words hit me like a *Floyd Mayweather* left hook.

"Tonight, you saved my life. I was going to do something I would've regretted forever. But after hearing you, everything changed. Thank you."

On the drive home, I couldn't stop thinking: How many of those kids would make the right choices? And how many would fall to the power of influence?

Now, I ask you the same question.

What choices have you made that you wish you could undo?

Maybe you took a job for the paycheck instead of your purpose. Maybe you're in a relationship you know isn't right, but leaving feels impossible. Or maybe you picked up a habit that's slowly destroying you. Sometimes, it's not even the big choices that weigh us down, it's the small, daily ones that pull us further from God little by little. The Bible makes it clear that we can't live in two worlds. **Joshua 24:15** puts it bluntly: *"Choose this day whom you will serve."*

It's easy to think we have time, that we can figure it out later. But **James 4:17** warns us, *"If anyone knows the good they ought to do and doesn't do it, it is sin."* The reality? Every decision either draws you toward God or pulls you further from Him. There is no neutral ground.

We all have a choice. We can hold on to bitterness, or we can pursue peace. **Colossians 3:15** urges us to "**let the peace of Christ rule in your hearts.**" We can stay the same, making excuses, or we can take action. **James 1:22** reminds us not to just listen to the Word but to do what it says.

It only takes one second to decide. One second to walk away from that toxic job. One second to leave that draining relationship. One second to say, **"God, I choose You."**

And here's the good news: no matter how far you've strayed, it's never too late. As long as you have breath in your lungs, you have the power to change.

But let's be real: change isn't easy. It takes courage. That's why God commanded Joshua, *"Be strong and courageous. Do not be afraid; do not be discouraged, for the Lord your God will be with you wherever you go."* (**Joshua 1:9**)

This isn't just about better decision-making. It's about war. The enemy is relentless, using distractions, temptations, and even people to pull you away from God. But here's the truth: the devil only has as much power as you give him.

It's time to take your power back. Choose God in everything you do. You won't always get it right, but stay on the narrow road: the one that leads to life. As **Matthew 7:14** reminds us, ***"But small is the gate and narrow the road that leads to life, and only a few find it."***

Surround yourself with people who push you toward Him. And if your choices have pulled you away, you already know what to do.

Take a moment. Look at your life. **Are your choices serving you, or are they serving God?**

Because at the end of the day, only you can answer that question.

Pray with me

Lord,

Thank You for Your love, grace, and mercy. I surrender my will to You today and ask for Your strength and wisdom in every decision I make. If my choices have pulled me away from You, I ask for forgiveness and the courage to turn back. Help me to trust You fully and align my heart with Your plans. Guide my steps and remind me that true peace comes from walking in Your ways. May my choices reflect Your goodness and bring glory to Your name.

In Jesus' name,
Amen.

Day 33

You Were Never Meant to Carry It Alone

Sometimes life will hit you so hard that you don't even know how to stand back up. There will be moments when your thoughts feels unbearable, when you're drowning in emotions you can't even explain. You'll look around for someone: anyone to talk to, but no one is there. Or worse, you convince yourself that even if they were, they wouldn't understand.

But God does.

I heard a quote that said, **"Sometimes when you're in a dark place, you think you've been buried, but actually, you've been planted."**

That darkness you feel? It's not your ending: it's the beginning of something greater.

I know that place. I've been there, trapped in a mind crowded with worries I couldn't escape, searching for answers to questions I couldn't even name. And the Bible calls it exactly what it is: *"the worries of this life."* **(Luke 8:14).**

If you haven't been there yet, trust me: you will. Life has a way of shaking everything you once thought was certain. But even in the uncertainty, God remains.

I've been in that place where the silence is so loud it suffocates you. Where you try to distract yourself, but nothing works. And when you finally decide to open your mouth and ask for help, no one answers.

But here's the truth: sometimes, God allows that silence because He's waiting for you to call on Him.

Before Jesus went to the cross, He withdrew to pray, knowing what was ahead. He fell on His face and cried out, ***"Father, if You are willing, take this cup from me; yet not my will, but Yours be done."*** (**Luke 22:42**).

And when He returned to His disciples: the people He trusted to stay awake and pray with Him, **they were asleep.**

Not because they didn't care. Not because they didn't love Him. But because they weren't meant to carry what only Jesus could carry.

God is waiting for you to come to Him, to surrender what you've been carrying for far too long. ***"Come to Me, all you who are weary and burdened, and I will give you rest."*** (**Matthew 11:28**).

The enemy wants to distract you. The moment you start stepping into what God has called you to do, **the challenges come**. The closer you get to God, the more your path changes. And with that change, some people and things will naturally fall away. **But don't be discouraged, the right people, the ones meant to walk with you, will stay.**

Some of you are holding onto things God has been telling you to release. You're clinging to people who were only meant for a season. You're holding onto past mistakes that God has already forgiven. You keep replaying situations you can't change. You carry guilt and shame when grace is waiting for you. You hold onto anger and unforgiveness, thinking it will make things right. Fear is keeping you from stepping into your calling. You're gripping onto a version of your life that no longer aligns with God's plan. You're relying on your own strength when God is asking you to surrender to His.

The enemy wants you to believe that letting go means losing. But in God's hands, letting go means making room. His plan is always better. Trust Him and step forward in faith.

"The Lord is close to the brokenhearted and saves those who are crushed in spirit." **(Psalm 34:18).**

God never promised an easy road. But He did promise you wouldn't have to walk it alone.

So when you feel lost in your thoughts: **talk to God**.
When people don't show up the way you expected: **talk to God.**
When you feel like you have nothing left: **talk to God**.

Because He is listening.

Pray with me

Father, in the Name of Jesus...

I lift up every person reading this right now. Lord, You see their struggles. You see their silent battles. You see the burdens they carry that no one else knows about. And right now, in this moment, I ask that You meet them exactly where they are.

Break every chain, Lord. Destroy every stronghold. Silence every lie the enemy has whispered in their ear.

Let them know that they are not alone. That they were never meant to carry this by themselves. That You are standing with them, holding them, loving them through every trial, every storm, every battle.

Father, I pray for breakthrough. For peace that surpasses all understanding. For strength to keep going even when it feels impossible.

Lord, You said in Your Word that "You will never leave us nor forsake us." So remind them today that You are right here. That even in their darkest hour, You are their light.

We surrender to You, God. We trust You. We say yes to Your will.

In Jesus' name,
Amen.

Day 34

The Leap That Changed Everything

What if I told you that God is trying to get your attention? Would you believe me? Do you know that He loves you deeply and longs for a relationship with you? And if you already walk with Him, He desires to draw you even closer.

I remember when my daughter was five years old. She used to stand on the second step from the bottom of the stairs while I stood in front of her with my arms stretched out, saying, **"Jump."** But I could see the hesitation in her eyes. She was afraid. So instead of pushing, I gently told her, **"Come closer,"** encouraging her to step down to the first step before jumping. And she did, not because she fully trusted me, but because the distance seemed smaller, safer.

Over time, she grew bolder. One step turned into two, then three, then four. And each time, she learned that no matter how far she jumped, **I would catch her**.

This is exactly what God desires for us. He wants us to trust Him, not just with the easy steps but with the ones that scare us. ***"Trust in the Lord with all your heart and lean not on*** *your own understanding"* (**Proverbs 3:5**). He is calling you to take a leap of faith, to surrender control, to stop hesitating. I know it feels terrifying at first: after all, you've been the one calling the shots in your life. But where has that led you?

Before I surrendered my life to Christ, I thought I had it all figured out. On the outside, I looked put together, but on the inside, there was a void, an emptiness I tried to ignore, cover up, or fill with temporary things. **But nothing worked.**

Because the truth is, **only God can fill the void inside of us**. No person, no achievement, no possession, no amount of success can satisfy that deep longing in your soul. *"My soul thirsts for God, for the living God"* (**Psalm 42:2**).

I didn't see it at the time, but I was drifting, lost in distractions, unaware that God was reaching out to me over and over again. He sent people: one, two, sometimes three, to get my attention. **But I ignored the signs**. I chalked everything up to coincidence, never realizing that God was calling me to something greater. Until one day, I couldn't ignore Him anymore.

Maybe you've felt that pull too: waking up in the middle of the night, burdened by thoughts you can't shake. Maybe you've felt an emptiness, a nudge, a whisper in your spirit. That isn't a coincidence. That is God. *"Behold, I stand at the door and knock. If anyone hears My voice and opens the door, I will come in"* (**Revelation 3:20**).

When I finally surrendered, God didn't reject me for my brokenness. He didn't turn me away because of my past mistakes. Instead, He embraced me, cleaned me up, and showed me a love unlike anything I had ever known. *"The Lord is close to*

the brokenhearted and saves those who are crushed in spirit"
(Psalm 34:18).

Like my daughter standing on the stairs, unsure whether to trust, I had to take that first leap of faith. And just like I caught her every time, God caught me.

And He will catch you too.

I am a living testimony of God's goodness. Everything I am today is because of Him. So, I'm telling you this: **God is calling you. Will you answer?**

Maybe He has already started removing people or things from your life to get your attention. Maybe He's stirring something inside of you that you can't ignore. **Don't wait any longer.**

Saying **"Yes"** to God doesn't mean you'll never stumble. It doesn't mean you'll always get it right. But it does mean that when you fall, He will pick you up. *"The steps of a good man are ordered by the Lord, and He delights in his way. Though he may stumble, he will not fall, for the Lord upholds him with His hand"* (Psalm 37:23-24).

So if you've been hesitant: if you've been waiting for the perfect moment, this is it. Say yes to Him today. Trust Him with your life, your future, your everything.

Because just like I stood at the bottom of those stairs, arms open wide, **God is standing before you now, waiting.**

Take the leap.

Pray with me

Heavenly Father,

I come before You right now, lifting up every person reading these words. Lord, You know their hearts. You know their struggles, their fears, and the burdens they carry. Father, I ask that You touch them in a way that only You can. Let them feel Your love, Your peace, and Your presence in their lives.

For those who don't know You yet, Lord, I pray that today will be the day they say yes to You. That they surrender their worries, their doubts, and their plans into Your hands. That they take the leap of faith, knowing that You will catch them.

For those who already walk with You but feel distant, remind them that You have never left. That You are always near, always waiting, always calling them back.

Thank You for Your unfailing love. Thank You for Your grace that meets us right where we are. And thank You for never giving up on us.

In Jesus' name,
Amen.

Day 35

A Simple Act of Love

You never truly know what another person is going through unless you take the time to talk to them.

Many of you know that my latest book, *The Hidden Exchange* was recently published. The love, support, and encouragement I've received from so many of you have meant the world to me: **thank you!** But what you may not know is that as excited as I was about finally releasing the book, my heart was focused on something much deeper: **helping and encouraging others**.

I don't write for recognition. I don't create for personal gain. I do it all for **God's glory**, because every gift He has given me belongs to Him. But beyond books and accomplishments, what truly moves me is this: **the silent battles people are fighting every day**. The ones we don't see on TV, read about in books, or scroll past on social media.

So let me ask you: **When was the last time you shared a kind word with someone: not because they did anything special, but simply because you were thinking about them?**

A simple word of encouragement can lift a soul in ways we may never fully understand. It costs nothing but could mean everything to someone in need.

People have told me how proud they are of me for writing books, and while I am grateful, my heart is always drawn to those who are struggling: the man holding a sign on the street corner, the mother at the grocery store counting change for a loaf of bread, the one battling depression, the sick lying in a hospital bed with no one to visit them. **That is where my heart is truly tested.**

I may not have everything, but what I do have, I will share, because that is how God created me. I don't give because I want something in return; I give because **God first loved me.** In a world filled with disappointment, people need to see a **glimmer of hope**, and that hope begins with you and me.

There are people waiting for your phone call, your text, your forgiveness, your encouragement. **Don't wait. Reach out.**

So often, we get caught up in our own world that we forget about others. But here's what I love about God: **He never forgets about us.** He promised, *"Never will I leave you; never will I forsake you."* **(Hebrews 13:5)**

Nothing: not hardship, not loss, not failure, not even our mistakes can separate us from His love **(Romans 8:38-39)**. **How humbling is that?** That the King of Kings would go to the Cross so that we could be free and have a relationship with our Heavenly Father!

So today, let me remind you:
- **You are more than a conqueror.**
- **You are a warrior.**
- **You are an overcomer.**
- **You can do anything God has called you to do.**

If no one has told you this today, **I am proud of you**. And if I were standing in front of you right now, I would give you the biggest hug, because maybe you need it. **And even if you don't, I guarantee you know someone who does.**

So here's my challenge for you today: **Reach out to someone you haven't spoken to in weeks, months, or even years. Tell them you're thinking about them.** Tell them you love them. Your words have the power to set them, and you: **free.**

You are here for a reason. Your life has meaning. And I believe in you.

If this is the first time you've heard someone say they are proud of you, **it won't be the last**. Every time you read this, let it be a reminder of how truly great you are.

And before you go any further, **do this one thing:**

Find a mirror. Look at yourself. **Tell yourself that you are proud of you. Tell yourself that you are loved.**

Jesus didn't go to the Cross for just you and me, He went to save the entire world. *"For God so loved the world that He gave His only begotten Son, that whosoever believes in Him shall not perish but have everlasting life."* (John 3:16)

What a sacrifice. We will never be able to repay Jesus for what He did for us, but we can use our lives to reflect His love to others. **Kindness costs nothing: but it is priceless.**

Pray with me

Heavenly Father,

Thank You for Your unconditional love. Thank You for reminding me that I am never alone, that You are always with me. Lord, help me to be a vessel of Your kindness. Open my eyes to those around me who need encouragement. Give me a heart that sees, ears that listen, and hands that serve. May my words bring life, and my actions reflect Your love. And when I grow weary, remind me that You are my strength.

I surrender my gifts, my time, and my heart to You, Lord. Let everything I do bring You glory.

In Jesus' name,
Amen.

Day 36

Bet On Yourself

When was the last time you truly took a chance on yourself? Not just thought about it, not just dreamed about it, but actually stood up and declared, **"I will no longer hold myself back!"** When was the last time you silenced the fear, ignored the doubts, and believed: really believed, that greatness is inside you because **God put it there?**

Life will throw distractions, detours, and delays your way. But at the end of the day, the biggest obstacle isn't life, it's you. The hesitation. The fear. The excuses. **Enough is enough**. When will you stop waiting for permission and start stepping boldly into what God has already called you to do?

Too many people hide, afraid to be seen, afraid to fail, afraid of what others might think. But let me make this clear: **you were not created to live small**. God placed something extraordinary inside of you. That passion you feel? That dream that won't let go? That vision that keeps you up at night? **It's not there by accident.** God entrusted it to you. So why are you burying it? Why are you playing it safe when you were meant to shake the world?

What is stopping you? Fear? Doubt? The voice in your head telling you you're not enough? That voice is **a lie**. God does not call the qualified, **He qualifies the called**. And you, my friend, **are called**. If you want change, then take action. If you want a new job, go after it. If you want to strengthen your faith, pursue God relentlessly. If you want to get healthy, start today. If you want to chase your dream, stop running in circles and run toward it with everything you've got.

And listen to me: f**aith is not passive**. Faith **moves**. Faith **acts**. Faith doesn't sit around waiting for the perfect moment, it creates the moment. **James 2:26** says, "*Faith without works is dead.*" You cannot just hope for a breakthrough. You must work for it. Pray, yes: but also move. Because nothing changes if you don't.

If we are not careful, we can speak things into existence that were never meant to be. There is a reason the Bible warns us that *"The tongue has the power of life and death"* **(Proverbs 18:21).** When we dwell on negative thoughts, when we repeat lies about ourselves, we give power to things that have no authority in our lives.

If I had listened to doubt, I would have never written six books. If I had listened to fear, I would have stayed in my comfort zone. But I didn't, and **neither should you**. Trusting God is the key. When He calls you, He equips you. **Philippians 4:13** declares, *"I can do all things through Christ who strengthens me."* That includes you. **So what are you waiting for?**

Right now: **yes, right now**, I challenge you to take one bold step. Write down your goal. Speak it out loud. Make the call.

Send the email. Take the leap. Move! Your breakthrough isn't in tomorrow, it's in what you do today.

The Bible says if you have faith the size of a mustard seed, you can move mountains **(Matthew 17:20)**. So move yours. Break out of the mindset that says, "Maybe later." No, right now. **Mark 11:24** says, *"Whatever you ask for in prayer, believe that you have received it, and it will be yours."* Believe it. Act on it. And watch God move in ways you never imagined.

Stop waiting for someone else to tell you **it's your time**. It is your time. Step into it. Own it. Live it. The world is waiting for you to rise.

Pray with me

Father God,

I refuse to live in fear any longer. I refuse to let doubt control me. Today, I step out in faith, believing that You have already equipped me for what You've called me to do. Strengthen me, guide me, and push me forward. I choose to stop waiting. I choose to act.

In Jesus' name,
Amen.

Day 37

Master Your Mind, Find Your Peace

Life's worries have the power to steal our joy, paralyze our progress, and cloud our future. But here's the truth: most of our struggles don't come from our circumstances. They come from our thoughts about them.

Think about it. When people say they have a problem, what do they really mean? If we break it down, 99% of what troubles us lives in our minds, shaped by our fears, doubts, and anxieties. Only 1% comes from the actual situation itself. Often, the real issue isn't the problem, it's the way we think about it.

We allow our thoughts to consume us, dictate our emotions, and control our decisions. But emotions, when left unchecked, can be deceptive. **Jeremiah 17:9** reminds us, *"The heart is deceitful above all things and beyond cure. Who can understand it?"* That means we can't trust every thought that enters our minds. Some of our thoughts are rooted in insecurity, fear, and false narratives that the enemy would love for us to believe.

If we are not careful, we can speak about a situation that isn't even true, yet give it life until it manifests. **Proverbs 23:7** tells us, *"As a man thinketh in his heart, so is he."* What you dwell on becomes your reality. This is why we must be intentional about aligning our thoughts with God's truth.

With everything shifting in the world, it's easy to feel backed into a corner, unsure of how we'll make it. Why? Because we've become dependent on things rather than the Source of all things: God. He tells us in **Matthew 6:31-32**, *"Do not worry, saying, 'What shall we eat?' or 'What shall we drink?'… Your heavenly Father knows that you need them."* Yet so many of us rely on man until we're desperate, then turn to God as a last resort. But God doesn't belong in a box: He is our ever-present help.

The enemy knows exactly how to manipulate our thoughts. **Genesis 3:1** describes the serpent as *"more crafty than any of the wild animals the Lord God had made."* His strategy has always been deception. When Cain was on the verge of sin, God warned him in **Genesis 4:7**, *"Sin is crouching at your door; it desires to have you, but you must rule over it."*

Even Jesus Himself called out the enemy's tactics. In **Matthew 16:23**, when Peter unknowingly spoke against God's plan, Jesus responded, *"Get behind me, Satan!"* Not because Peter was the enemy, but because the enemy was trying to work through him. Satan will use every trick in his arsenal to deceive you. But here's the truth: **the only power he has over you is the power you give him.** Take your power back. Speak life over every situation and watch God move.

The truth is, most problems are solved with less, not more. Less overthinking. Less worrying. Less trying to control things beyond our reach. **Philippians 4:6-7** tells us, *"Do not be* *anxious about anything, but in every situation, by prayer and petition, with thanksgiving, present your requests to God. And the peace of God, which transcends all understanding, will guard your hearts and your minds in Christ Jesus."*

Sometimes, the answer isn't in doing more, it's in being still. If you can't change it, stop obsessing over it. If you can't fix the past, let it go. The past is a closed door, and you hold the key to your future. Make peace with yesterday, stop worrying about tomorrow, and embrace today. *"This is the day that the Lord has made; let us rejoice and be glad in it."* (Psalm 118:24)

One of the biggest battles we fight is in our own minds. Our thoughts can either build us up or tear us down. That's why it's so important to take control of them. Not everything that crosses your mind is true. Not every thought deserves your attention. **2 Corinthians 10:5** urges us to *"take captive every thought to make it obedient to Christ."* That means filtering out the lies, rejecting the negativity, and choosing to believe what God says about you.

You are an overcomer. You are a warrior. And the peace you're searching for? It doesn't come from the world. It comes from God.

So the next time your thoughts try to betray you, the next time anxiety tells you that you're not enough, the next time fear tries to hold you back: Stop. Pray. Surrender it to God. The only peace you truly need is His peace.

Don't let worry consume your life. It's a thief. A destroyer. A liar.

Now, ask yourself: what has your mind told you today that isn't true?

Pray with me

Heavenly Father,

Thank You for renewing my mind daily. Forgive me for the times I have let my thoughts control me instead of trusting in You. Help me take captive every thought that is not from You. Fill me with Your peace, the peace that surpasses all understanding. When my mind is restless, remind me that You are my refuge. Let my thoughts align with Your truth, and let my heart rest in Your promises. I surrender my worries to You.

In Jesus' name,
Amen.

Day 38

Your Gift, God's Glory

It's been nearly a week since my last blog, and I'm sure some of you have wondered what was going on. Why hadn't I sent out my regular posts? I took a week off to dedicate myself to completing my latest book, and I'm happy to announce that it's finished and ready to be published: thank God!

Sometimes, we have to set things aside to focus on what God has placed in our hearts. That brings me to today's message. Too often, we pour our time and energy into everything and everyone else, making them a priority while treating our own calling as an afterthought. But let me ask you this: when was the last time you truly invested in yourself? When was the last time you nurtured the gift God placed inside you?

For me, these past seven days were an investment. I made a commitment to finish my book before writing another blog. And let me tell you, it wasn't easy. I love writing these blogs. I love encouraging people and pouring into others. But I was reminded of something my daughter said when she was just eight years old.

One day, she saw me stop everything I was doing to help someone else with their project. Later, she looked at me with innocent but wise eyes and asked, "Dad, why do you always help everyone with their stuff when you have your own stuff to do? Nobody helps you with your stuff, so maybe you should stop helping all the time and just work on your stuff."

Her words hit me hard. She was right. Sometimes, we need to give ourselves the same dedication that we so freely give to others. And that's not selfish, that's stewardship. God has entrusted you with gifts, talents, and dreams. If you keep putting them on hold, how can you fully walk in the purpose He has for you?

Each of us has a unique gift that, when nurtured, brings fulfillment, joy, and purpose. More than that, it becomes a blessing to others and draws people closer to God. **Romans 12:6** reminds us, *"We have different gifts, according to the grace given to each of us."* Your gift isn't just for you, it's meant to impact lives. But it can only do that if you invest in it.

For me, writing is my calling. Whether it's refining my manuscript, working with an editor, or ensuring every word carries purpose: I pour into this gift because I know God has called me to it. And having a trusted friend design my book covers is just another way God surrounds me with people who help bring the vision to life.

Having a strong support system matters. When you're running on empty, you need people in your life who will uplift you, encourage you, and remind you why you started. But even if no one else understands your journey, God does. He is your greatest source of strength and wisdom.

So, what about you? What's the gift you've been putting on hold? What's the dream God placed in your heart that you keep pushing aside? Maybe it's your job, your family, or other responsibilities. And while those things are important, you can't pour from an empty cup. Investing in yourself doesn't mean neglecting others, it means ensuring you're equipped to give them your best.

1 Timothy 4:14 says, ***"Do not neglect your gift, which was given you through prophecy when the body of elders laid their hands on you."*** God has given you something special: something the world needs. Maybe it's singing, designing, mentoring youth, starting a business, or writing. Whatever it is, it's time to stop making excuses and start making room for what God has placed inside you.

This life is not a dress rehearsal: there's no coming back for a do-over. The time to step into your calling is now. **Ecclesiastes 9:10** says, ***"Whatever your hand finds to do, do it with all your might."*** God has been calling you: are you ready to answer?

If this spoke to you, I challenge you to take one step today toward investing in yourself and your God-given gift. Whether it's setting aside time to plan, taking a class, or simply praying for direction: do something that moves you closer to your purpose.

Pray with me

Lord,

Thank You for the gifts and dreams You've placed inside me. Forgive me for the times I've put them aside and made everything else a priority over the purpose You've given me. Today, I choose to invest in the calling You have placed on my life. Give me courage when I'm afraid, strength when I'm weary, and clarity when I'm unsure. Surround me with people who will support and encourage me. Let everything I do bring glory to You and draw others closer to You.

In Jesus' name,
Amen.

Day 39

Activate Your God-Given Gifts

If you have a dream moving inside you, calling to be awakened, or a passion that won't let go, whatever you do: **do not give up**. Don't abandon your mission just because it hasn't happened yet. Don't push it aside because no one else sees it. And don't bury it just because others fail to believe in it.

The graveyard is full of untapped potential, dreams never pursued, talents never developed, and ideas that never took flight. **Don't let that be your story.**

I remember speaking at a conference full of young people, asking each one what they dreamed of becoming. Their aspirations were big: lawyers, doctors, NBA players, business owners, police officers, and politicians. Then, I turned to their parents and asked if they knew their children's dreams. Not a single hand went up.

I don't share this to criticize parents but to inspire greatness, not just in the young but in everyone. Greatness isn't reserved for a select few; **it's in all of us**. Sometimes, the people who doubt your dreams are the very ones who never dared to believe in their own. Misery loves company, but success and failure both begin in the same place: **the mind**.

If you believe you'll fail, failure is waiting. If you believe you'll succeed, success is already preparing to meet you. The Bible says, *"With man this is impossible, but with God all things are possible"* (Matthew 19:26).

Many people wait for opportunities to fall into their laps, wasting valuable time that could be spent investing in their God-given purpose. There are 168 hours in a week. We spend much of that working, handling responsibilities, and sleeping. But what about the unaccounted hours? How are you using them? How much time are you dedicating to sharpening your skills, developing your gifts, and pursuing your purpose?

Personally, I strive to invest in myself every day; whether through writing, reading, spending time with God, exercising, or creating something meaningful. I keep moving forward.

Stop waiting for validation from others. Stop sharing your dreams with everyone, because not everyone is in your corner. The next thing you create, don't announce it until it's done. Jesus Himself taught, *"Do not let your left hand know what your right hand is doing"* (Matthew 6:3).

If you don't yet know what you are great at, **ask God** to reveal your purpose. Because when you find your purpose, you'll find exactly what you were created to do.

Each of us was designed with a unique ability to impact the world and draw people closer to God. If your goal is solely personal satisfaction and worldly gain, it will never fulfill you. But if your goal is to glorify God with the talents He has given you, then your gift will make room for you **(Proverbs 18:16)**.

Stop wasting time. Time is one thing you can never get back. If you're feeling discouraged, shake off the doubt and move forward. Everything you need to succeed is already within you: you just have to dig deep and ask God for the courage to use it for His glory.

Some of you carry million-dollar ideas that God planted in you before you were born. Others have talents that could change the world but are too afraid to step out in faith. Some of you feel stuck in jobs that drain your soul, yet fear has paralyzed you. If no one has ever told you this before, let me be the first: **You were created for greatness.** Your light was meant to shine.

The longer you wait, the easier it becomes to put it off indefinitely. Stop hesitating. If you want to go back to school: do it. If you want to write that book: start today. If you want to change your career: take the first step. If you want to improve your health: begin now.

Great victories come through great challenges. David didn't just defeat Goliath: he believed that God could do it through him. Moses didn't just part the Red Sea: he allowed God to work through him. Every miracle in the Bible came through a willing and obedient heart, knowing that it was God, not man, accomplishing the impossible.

What's stopping you from stepping into your greatness? **Mark 11:24** says, *"Therefore I tell you, whatever you ask for in prayer, believe that you have received it, and it will be yours."*

What are you asking for? What are you believing for?

It's time to take action and trust God to lead the way. If you don't know where He is leading, stop, pray, and seek His wisdom. **James 1:5** reminds us, *"If any of you lacks wisdom,* *you should ask God, who gives generously to all without finding fault, and it will be given to you.* "But when you ask, do not doubt, because the one who doubts is like a wave tossed by the wind.

Too often, God gives us direction, yet we run to others for confirmation instead of standing on His word. Be careful who you seek counsel from, because the wrong voices can lead you astray. Remember what happened in the Garden of Eden when Eve entertained the wrong voice. When in doubt, s**eek God first**, not just in some areas, but in **all areas of your life**.

Everything you do in life can be activated by your faith in God. So here's my challenge to you: Stop complaining. Stop comparing. Trust that God has amazing plans for **YOUR** life. Get in your own lane and run the race designed for you. Don't become a copy of someone else: become the best version of who God created you to be.

The world needs authenticity, not imitation. Jesus is calling you to follow Him. Are you ready?

Pray with me

Heavenly Father,

Thank You for the gifts and dreams You have placed inside of me. Help me to trust You fully, to step out in faith, and to move forward with confidence. Remove any fear, doubt, or hesitation that keeps me from pursuing the purpose You have for my life. Lord, I surrender my plans to You. Give me the strength to endure challenges and the wisdom to recognize opportunities. May everything I do bring glory to Your name.

In Jesus' name, Amen.

Day 40

What Truly Matters

The late, great martial artist Bruce Lee, one of the world's most brilliant minds, once said, **"The great mistake is to anticipate the outcome of the engagement; you ought not to be thinking of whether it ends in victory or defeat. Let nature take its course, and your tools will strike at the right moment."**

In essence, he was saying that focusing too much on the outcome; whether winning or losing, can prevent you from responding effectively in the moment. But when you let go of expectations and trust the process, your actions will come naturally, and you'll strike at the right time.

This reminds me of what **Ecclesiastes 7:8** says: *"Better is the end of a thing than its beginning, and the patient in spirit is better than the proud in spirit."*

Life isn't predictable. It's not a crystal ball that lets us see into the future, nor a magic wand that makes our problems disappear. Every day is different, just as no two people are the same. And if you've lived long enough, you know that life brings both victories and setbacks. But it's not about where you start:

it's about where you finish. The key is trusting that God is in control, even when the path isn't clear.

Yet, so many of us carry burdens we were never meant to bear. We're weighed down by worries: about family, finances, health, work, school, and everything in between. When life overwhelms you, what do you do? Do you try to handle it all on your own, or do you surrender it to God?

"Cast your cares on the Lord and He will sustain you; He will never let the righteous be shaken." (Psalm 55:22)

I learned this the hard way. I remember my first college basketball game, something I had trained for relentlessly. But instead of trusting my preparation, **I let doubt creep in**. I feared I wouldn't perform well, that I'd turn the ball over too much, that my hard work wouldn't show.

The night before, I couldn't sleep. I kept replaying every possible scenario: what I would do, what I wouldn't do, how many shots I'd take, whether we'd win or lose. **My mind was consumed with the what-ifs.**

Yet, when I finally stepped onto the court, something shifted. It was as if I belonged there. Every pass, every shot: it all came together. Looking back, I wish I had known Bruce Lee's words back then.

But **more importantly**, I wish I had understood what I know now: **We serve a God who doesn't operate on autopilot. He is intentional in every moment.**

"Do not worry about your life, what you will eat or drink; or about your body, what you will wear. Is not life more than food, and the body more than clothes?" (Matthew 6:25)

Instead of overanalyzing every step, **God calls us to seek Him first and trust that He has already made a way.**

When Jesus fasted for 40 days, the enemy tried to shake Him. The devil tempted Him three times: first with food, then with power, and finally with control over the kingdoms of the world.

But Jesus didn't waver. He responded with truth: *"Away from me, Satan! For it is written: 'Worship the Lord your God, and serve Him only.'"* (Matthew 4:10)

We may not bow to the devil, **but how often do we bow to fear?** How often do we let our circumstances, struggles, and doubts have more power than our faith?

But God wants us to **choose Him above everything else**. No matter how big the problem seems, bring it to Him. You were never meant to carry it alone.

"Come to me, all you who are weary and burdened, and I will give you rest." (Matthew 11:28)

"A person's steps are directed by the Lord. How then can anyone understand their own way?" (Proverbs 20:24)

This verse reminds us that God is ultimately in control of our lives. Because of this, we won't always understand the reasons behind what we face. **But trusting God means knowing that His plan is greater than our limited perspective.**

We may not always have the answers, but one thing is certain: **If you trust God, you can never go wrong.**

So, as you go through your day, remember this:

- If you can't control it, don't let it control you.
- Instead of worrying about what you **cannot** control, **create something great**.
- When you trust **God's approval over man's**, you walk in His strength and power.

God will always show you what you need to see: sometimes through others, sometimes through the Spirit, but always in His perfect time.

Pray with me

Lord,

Thank You for being our refuge in times of uncertainty. You remind us that we do not have to carry the weight of this world on our shoulders because You are our strength. Lord, help us to trust You fully, to release what we cannot control, and to walk in faith rather than fear. When doubt creeps in, let Your Word be our guide. When we feel overwhelmed, remind us that You hold our future in Your hands. We surrender our worries, our plans, and our desires to You, knowing that Your ways are higher than ours. Let us rest in Your promises, walk in Your peace, and trust in Your perfect timing. May everything we do bring You glory.

In Jesus' name, Amen.

Day 41

The Cost of Choosing God

If you know anything about chess, you know it's a game of strategy, patience, and sacrifice. Sometimes, you have to let go of certain pieces to protect what's most important. One wrong move can cost you the game. But sometimes, the hardest sacrifices lead to the greatest victories.

The same is true when you choose to walk with God.

Some relationships will change. Some people will walk away. And at times, you'll feel like you're standing alone. But you're not. God is with you, guiding you through every move.

Think about a chessboard. It represents life, with each square symbolizing different situations and choices. Every piece moves differently, just like the people and things in your life. Some are meant to stay, like the king, **which represents your faith, the core of who you are**. Others? They're only with you for a season. And just like in chess, sometimes, you have to let go of certain pieces to win the game.

When you decide to truly follow God, your values start to change. The conversations you used to enjoy don't feel the same. The places you used to go don't bring the same excitement. You start craving something deeper, something real. And as you grow, some people won't understand. Some will distance themselves. Others will make you feel like you're "too much" or "too different."

It's not because you think you're better than them, it's because you're moving in a different direction. **This is the cost of choosing God.**

I remember when I got serious about my faith. I let go of certain habits, and before I knew it, the people closest to me started drifting away. My circle got so small that I started questioning myself.

"Am I doing something wrong?"
"Should I just go back to how things were?"
"Is it really worth it?"

For a moment, I thought about compromising: about dimming my light just to fit in. But then God reminded me: **I wasn't walking the wrong path, I was just walking a different one.**

But here's the truth: whatever you lose in the process was never meant to stay.

The Bible says in **Luke 9:23**, *"Whoever wants to be my disciple must deny themselves and take up their cross daily and follow me."*

Sometimes, separation is necessary for elevation.

Maybe for you, it's not just relationships. Maybe it's a habit, a mindset, a job, or a comfort zone that you know isn't leading you closer to God. And letting go of it? That's not easy.

But choosing God means choosing obedience, even when it's uncomfortable. It means trusting that whatever you release, **He will replace with something greater.**

Isaiah 55:8-9 reminds us, *"For my thoughts are not your thoughts, neither are your ways my ways," declares the Lord. "As the heavens are higher than the earth, so are my ways higher than your ways and my thoughts than your thoughts."*

It's not rejection: it's redirection.

If you're in a season where it feels like you're losing more than you're gaining, hold on to this: God is never subtracting, He's making room for more.

You may have lost some things, but you've gained something far greater: **His presence, His guidance, and His purpose for your life.** And that's worth more than anything you had to leave behind.

Pray with me

Lord,

I know that following You comes with sacrifice. Help me trust You when I have to let go. Give me the strength to walk away from anything that pulls me from You, even when it's hard. Fill my heart with peace, knowing that Your plan is greater than my own. Align me with people who will help me grow in You, and remove anything that stands in the way of my purpose. I choose You above all else.

In Jesus' name,
Amen.

Day 42

God's Timing, Not Ours

No matter how talented you are, if you are in the wrong place and not aligned with God, you will be ineffective.

Over the past seven weeks, I've been working on finalizing the edits of my newest book, The *Hidden Exchange*, and I've found it challenging to get it done. The book is already written, and the first round of professional edits has been completed. Now, I'm in the final stages, but I keep critiquing it more than I probably should. I want it to be excellent.

With my day-to-day responsibilities, attending my daughter's high school basketball games, staying in the presence of God, and handling life's demands: I realized something important: In order to maximize my efforts, I need a strategic and uninterrupted plan to maintain my focus, because anything worth praying for is worth working for.

But sometimes, despite our best efforts, life seems to slow us down. Or maybe, just maybe, it isn't life at all: it's God repositioning us.

Originally, The *Hidden Exchange* was set to release in January 2025. But as time passed, I kept asking myself, Why is this taking so long? The book is already written and edited. And then, I heard God say, That was your plan, not Mine.

Proverbs 16:1 reminds us: *"We humans make plans, but the Lord has the final word."*

That verse stopped me in my tracks. We can make all the plans we want, but God determines the timing. It doesn't mean our plans won't come to pass, it means God decides when, not man. When I realized I was putting too much pressure on myself, I had to ask: **Am I doing this in my own power, or am I allowing God to lead?**

Because here's the truth: Sometimes, God wants to reposition us for His glory.

What are you passionate about? Have you ever poured your heart into something, felt so close to the finish line, and then, suddenly: you were redirected?

Maybe that redirection isn't a setback. Maybe it's God still growing you. Maybe He's stretching you, teaching you that it's not just about reaching the goal, but about what comes with it.

For me, writing wasn't just about finishing the book, it was about preparing for what comes with it. What if I released it too soon without a clear strategy? What if God wanted me to wait because there was something else He needed me to do first?

Sometimes, delays aren't obstacles: **they're divine setups.**

What about you? Has God ever shifted something in your life? Maybe it's a career, a relationship, a location, or a passion. You thought you were headed in one direction, but suddenly, He changed the course. If so, trust Him.

Proverbs 3:5-6 says, *"Trust in the Lord with all your heart and lean not on your own understanding; in all your ways submit to Him, and He will make your paths straight."*

When we surrender our goals, dreams, and desires to God, He leads us to something greater than we could ever achieve on our own. The world may promise success through hard work and ambition, but true success comes from alignment with God. A life with Him is greater than all the riches, honor, and accolades in the world without Him.

So, submit your plans to Him. Trust His timing. And when He repositions you, follow His lead. Because where He takes you will always be greater than where you thought you were going.

Pray with me

Lord,

Lord, thank You for Your perfect timing. Help me to trust You even when I don't understand the delays. I surrender my plans, dreams, and ambitions to You. If You are repositioning me, let me embrace it with faith, knowing that Your ways are always higher. Teach me patience, humility, and unwavering trust in You.

In Jesus' name,
Amen.

Day 43

When Love Speaks Louder Than Words

What if the very thing you've been searching for has been within you all along? What if God isn't asking you to find it **but to awaken it?**

I once heard a quote: **"If everything around you seems dark, look again. You may be the light."** Life changes: hour by hour, moment by moment, but one thing remains constant: **God**. So, here's the question: How deep is your love? Not just in words, but in action. When people encounter you, do they walk away better, encouraged, or unchanged?

I remember when my daughter was in sixth grade, and she asked me if she could get a dog. Now, as a parent, I knew that dogs require a lot of attention, time, and care. But instead of saying **"no,"** I offered a challenge. **"If you can stay on the honor roll from sixth to eighth grade, I'll get you a dog."**

She looked at me, smiled, and without missing a beat, said, **"OK, deal!"** Then, with the brightest smile, she reached out her pinky and said, **"Pinky promise?"**

I wrapped my pinky around hers, sealing the promise.

The next three years passed, and at the end of her eighth-grade year, I picked her up from school, just like I always did. But this time, there was something different about her smile. It was wider, more knowing. As she got into the truck, she asked me, **"Dad, you're a man of your word, right?"**

I paused, wondering what she was up to. After she buckled up, she handed me an envelope. Her smile kept growing. I opened the envelope, and there it was: the confirmation that she had maintained the honor roll for all three years. She worked for it, stayed disciplined, and patiently waited. Now, it was my turn to keep my promise. Two months later, we brought home a mini Australian Shepherd.

Why do I share this story? Because love, like faith, is about more than just words. It requires action. **James 2:17** reminds us, **"Faith without works is dead."** Similarly, love without action is empty. Words are powerful, but what are they worth if they're not followed by deeds?

Niccolò Machiavelli once said, **"Everyone sees what you appear to be; few experience what you really are."** People often judge based on what they see. But true love is shown through what we do, not just what we say.

Take my daughter's dog, for example. The dog can't speak, but her actions speak volumes. Every time she sees my daughter, her joy is undeniable: her wagging tail, the happy barks, the way she leaps to greet her. God created animals this way, perhaps to teach us that love isn't just spoken; it's demonstrated.

So, I ask you: What does your love look like?

God set the ultimate example: ***"For God so loved the world that He gave His only begotten Son."*** (**John 3:16**) If that's not love in action, I don't know what is. And in **1 Corinthians 13**, we learn more about what love is: it's patient, kind, humble, and forgiving. When I read these verses, I ask myself: Am I walking in this kind of love?

I know love isn't always easy. Sometimes, it's hard to love others—or even ourselves. We may carry past hurts that make forgiveness feel impossible. But Jesus didn't just suggest we love one another; He commanded it. ***"Love one another as I have loved you."*** (**John 13:34**)

The Bible also tells us that ***"perfect love casts out fear"*** (**1 John 4:18**). That perfect love is only found in God, and as we remain in Him, we are empowered to love, not just with words, but through our actions.

I'll be the first to admit, my love walk isn't perfect. I'm not always patient. I don't always put others first. But love, like faith, is a journey. It doesn't happen overnight, just like you don't plant a seed today and expect to eat its fruit tomorrow. It takes time, effort, and a heart that's willing to grow.

But God knows our struggles. And He gives us opportunities every day to practice love in action. The next time you're frustrated in traffic, extend patience. The next time someone wrongs you, choose grace. The next time you see someone hurting, offer kindness.

Love is the antidote. ***"Love covers a multitude of sins."*** (**1 Peter 4:8**) If love has the power to cover sin, just imagine what it can heal in our daily lives.

And if you ever doubt how much you're loved, remember **Romans 8:38-39**: nothing in all creation can separate us from the love of Christ.

God doesn't hold our past against us, so why do we hold onto the offenses of others? Even while hanging on the cross, Jesus said, ***"Father, forgive them."*** If He can love like that, so can we.

So, let's make the first move. Love deeply. Forgive freely. Extend grace daily. None of us are perfect, but all of us need love.

Pray with me

Lord,

Thank You for loving me, even when I fall short. Teach me to love as You love: patient, kind, and forgiving. Help me to put my faith into action, to love not just with words but through my deeds. I surrender my heart to You and ask that You use me to be a light in someone's darkness. Thank You for never letting anything separate me from Your love.

In Jesus' name,
Amen.

Your Story Is Bigger Than One Chapter

I don't know about you, but I'm a sports fan. From basketball to football to boxing: you name it, and I'll probably watch it. OK, maybe not every sport. But over the weekend, I caught the Baltimore Ravens vs. Buffalo Bills game. If you saw it, you know it was one of those nail-biters that had you on the edge of your seat.

The Ravens were on the verge of tying it up. Their quarterback threw what should have been a perfect pass to one of their most reliable receivers. But then, it happened. He dropped the ball. Just like that, they lost by two points.

The end result? Instant blame. People pointed fingers at the receiver, as if the entire loss was his fault. I'm sure he felt it: criticism from fans, from the media, maybe even from those closest to him. And I wouldn't be surprised if he blamed himself too.

But here's the truth: the game wasn't decided by one play. Football is a team sport. When I played basketball, it was always about the team: winning or losing as a unit. No single player should carry all the credit or all the blame.

In life, we can sometimes feel like it's all on us. We mess up, or something goes wrong, and we feel like we're the reason everything's falling apart. But let me tell you, you're not alone in this.

Let me share a story I once heard, a story that made me stop and think. It's one of those timeless lessons that I still carry with me today.

A man, overwhelmed by life's struggles, called out to the Lord, **"Lord, this cross is too much for me to carry."** The Lord, full of compassion, replied, **"My child, if it's too much, leave your cross in that room. Walk through the next door and pick the one you think will be lighter."**

The man, feeling a little relieved, did what he was told. As he entered the room, he saw crosses of all sizes: some so large they seemed to touch the sky. He searched, carefully navigating through the towering crosses, until he found a smaller one leaning against the wall. **"I'll take this one,"** he said.

The Lord smiled gently and said, **"That's the cross you brought in."**

That story has stuck with me. So often, we look at other people's struggles and think theirs must be easier than ours. But the truth is, we can never truly know what someone else is dealing with.

Instead of placing blame on ourselves or others, we need to remember we don't have to face it alone. **God didn't create us to handle life's challenges by ourselves.**

Matthew 11:28-30 reminds us, *"Come to me, all you who are weary and burdened, and I will give you rest. Take my yoke upon you and learn from me, for I am gentle and humble in heart, and you will find rest for your souls. For my yoke is easy and my burden is light."* Jesus doesn't want us to carry our struggles alone. He wants us to give them to Him.

And in **Psalm 55:22**, we're told: *"Cast your cares on the Lord and He will sustain you; He will never let the righteous be shaken."* God promises to hold us up, even when we feel like we can't stand anymore.

To the Baltimore Ravens receiver who dropped the ball: don't let this one mistake define you. You were an important part of your team's success. And to anyone else who feels like they've failed, remember this: You are so much more than your mistakes. **Stand tall**.

When life feels overwhelming, don't try to navigate it alone. Surrender your struggles to God. Ask for His help. And stop blaming yourself or others for every mistake. Life isn't about one moment; it's about the bigger picture, the journey you're on with God.

Take a moment to reflect on what you're wrestling with. Is it guilt? Fear? Being perfect? Write it down, and then, in prayer, give it all to God. Let Him replace your struggles with His peace.

Pray with me

Lord,

Thank You for being my refuge when life gets difficult. I come to You today, burdened with worries. I lay them at Your feet, trusting You to sustain me. Help me remember that my mistakes don't define me. Your love and grace are what shape me. Please give me the strength to move forward with courage and faith.

Thank You for always walking with me, even when the path feels too hard. I trust You to guide me, protect me, and renew my spirit.

In Jesus' name,
Amen.

Day 45

The Courage to Choose

Every decision we make, or avoid: has the power to pull us closer to our destiny or push us further away. The same is true of the people we allow into our lives. Some people build us up and help us fulfill God's purpose; others tear us down and distract us from His plan. Here's the challenge: can you tell the difference?

After college, I fell in with a group of tough, street-smart guys who I thought cared about me. We were thick as thieves, and I felt like I finally belonged. But deep down, I knew their choices didn't align with what I believed. Still, I stayed, because they were like family, and loyalty ran deep.

Over time, though, I realized the truth: we weren't walking the same path. Their values didn't line up with mine, and their influence could lead me to a place I never wanted to be. It was one of the hardest decisions I've ever made, but I severed ties with them. That moment changed everything. It was painful, but it also opened the door to something greater. It was through that decision that I found Christ, and the peace I had been searching for my whole life.

The Bible offers countless examples of people whose wrong connections led to their downfall. Take Samson and Delilah: Samson was one of the strongest men to ever live, but he lost his strength, and ultimately his life: because of someone who betrayed him. **Not everyone who smiles at you is happy to see you. And sometimes, the relationships we're holding onto are the very ones God has been telling us to release.**

Think about something in your life that you know shouldn't be there. Maybe it's a habit, a mindset, or even a relationship. You know it doesn't bring you peace. You know it pulls you further from God. Yet you keep holding onto it, hoping it will somehow work out. But here's the truth: you cannot pour new wine into old wineskins. If you want to step into the next chapter of your life, you have to let go of what's holding you back.

Walking the narrow path is about choosing God's way over the world's. It's about standing firm in your values, even when it's uncomfortable or unpopular. It means letting go of toxic connections and habits that don't align with God's plan for your life. It means silencing the opinions of others when they conflict with God's voice.

Jesus Himself reminds us of the narrow path in **Matthew 7:13-14**: *"Enter through the narrow gate. For wide is the gate and broad is the road that leads to destruction, and many enter through it. But small is the gate and narrow the road that leads to life, and only a few find it."*

It's not easy. Fear often holds us back: fear of being alone, fear of the unknown, or fear of what others might think. But **Joshua 1:9** reminds us, *"Be strong and courageous. Do not be afraid; do not be discouraged, for the Lord your God will be with you wherever you go."* God's plans for you are good, and

He promises never to leave you. Trust Him enough to take that first step onto the narrow path. He will guide you toward the abundant life He's prepared for you.

Take this moment to reflect on your life. **Are the people, habits, and mindsets shaping your journey pushing you closer to God, or pulling you away?**

Living with purpose as a leader of your own choices requires courage. It means letting go of what's easy for what truly matters. God doesn't want perfection: He wants you to be intentional. **When you trust Him, even in the hardest moments, you can step boldly into the amazing life He has for you.**

Let go of what's holding you back. Trust God to replace it with something greater. **God's light is already within you: it's time to let it shine.**

Pray with me

Lord,

Thank You for calling me to live with purpose. Help me discern the relationships, habits, and mindsets that no longer serve Your plan for my life. Give me the courage to walk the narrow path, even when it's difficult, and the faith to trust Your guidance above all else. Lord, fill me with Your Spirit, strengthen me, and lead me as I step boldly into the purpose You've prepared for me. Thank You for always being with me and for never leaving my side.

In Jesus' name,
Amen.

Day 46

When Fear Meets Faith, God Shows Up

What's on your mind right now? Is there a burden so heavy it feels impossible to share? Maybe it's a fear that keeps creeping in, or a problem you just can't shake. Maybe it's something you've carried for a long time: a broken relationship, the pain of loss, or doubt whispering that you're not enough or that God has forgotten you.

Here's the truth: no one is exempt from life's challenges. **Everyone** faces struggles, and none of us have it all figured out. But here's what I want you to know: **you don't have to face it alone**.

Let me share a story with you:

When I was in sixth grade, something happened that I'll never forget. It started like any other day. I was sitting in homeroom, talking with a few classmates, when the door swung open.

In walked someone I thought was a friend. But this time, he wasn't alone. He had a group of other sixth-grade boys behind him: kids with reputations for being tough.

He headed straight for my desk. The room went silent. I can still feel how the silence magnified every step he took.

When he got to me, he leaned down, looked me in the eye, and said loud enough for everyone to hear: "I'm going to fight you after school."

I laughed nervously, hoping he was kidding. "Yeah, okay," I said, trying to brush it off. But then he shoved me. Hard.

That's when I knew, it wasn't a joke.

The rest of the day passed in a blur. I couldn't focus on anything the teacher said. All I could think about was the final bell, the schoolyard, and what might happen.

When the last bell rang, my stomach sank. I grabbed my bag and headed out to the schoolyard, pretending to be calm even though my heart was pounding.

I stood there for what felt like forever, but he never showed up. Maybe he'd forgotten.

But as I started walking home, I heard someone calling my name. I turned around, and there he was. Only now, he wasn't alone. He had four other guys with him. They were laughing, pointing, and heading straight for me. My worst fear was staring me in the face. Without thinking, I ran as fast as I could. I didn't stop until I was home. When I walked inside, my older brother was sitting on the couch, watching TV. He glanced up and immediately knew something was wrong. "What happened?" he asked.

I shook my head, trying to play it off, but he wasn't buying it. He kept asking until I finally broke down and told him everything. When I finished, he didn't say a word. He just stood up, laced up his sneakers, and walked out the door. Ten minutes later, he came back. I was still pacing my room, too scared to go outside.

"You can go out now," he said.

"What do you mean?" I asked, confused.

"It's handled," he said simply.

I didn't know what he did or said, but I knew this: the fear that had gripped me all day was gone. My brother had stepped in for me, and because of that, I could finally breathe again.

That's what God does for us. Whatever you're facing today, God sees it. He knows the fear, the doubt, and the burdens you're carrying. And just like my brother, He's ready to step in and take care of it for you. He's not just watching from a distance: He's right here, helping you every step of the way.

The Bible says, ***"Cast all your cares on Him, for He cares for you"*** (1 Peter 5:7). God is with you, ready to fight for you and give you the strength to face what's ahead. He gets the glory for every victory, and He's the one who gives you the strength to overcome.

Fear has a way of making us feel stuck, like there's no way out. But God is bigger than your fear. He's bigger than the problem you're facing, and He's not going to leave you to figure it out on your own. His power is limitless, and His love is unshakable.

The same God who parted the Red Sea, who shut the mouths of lions, and who raised Jesus from the dead: **that same God is on your side.** You can trust Him. You can rest in Him. And when you do, fear has to go. Because fear cannot stand in the presence of our mighty God.

Life is hard, but you don't have to do it alone. God is with you, ready to carry whatever is troubling you and fight your battles. Trust that He's bigger than your struggles and that He's already at work in your life. And remember: you are never alone. **God is always with you.**

Pray with me

Heavenly Father,

You see what I'm going through. You know my fears, my worries, and the burdens I'm carrying. Lord, I give it all to You right now. I trust that You are bigger than my struggles and that Your plans for me are good. Thank You for loving me and for never leaving me. Help me to walk in Your peace and confidence, knowing You're always with me.

In Jesus' name,
Amen.

Day 47

God's Greatest Investment

If you had the opportunity to help someone, knowing you'd get nothing in return, would you still do it? Think about that for a moment. Imagine giving, and giving, and giving: never seeing a return on your investment. How would you feel?

Now, let's shift that question. How many times has God poured into your life, given you gifts, talents, opportunities, only for you to hold back? To never give back, to never answer His call?

One morning, on my way to work, I was going up the escalator when I turned and spotted one of my coworkers at the bottom. I smiled. She smiled back. That was it. Nothing deep, just a passing moment.

Later that day, during my lunch break, I headed downstairs to the gym connected to my office. I often used that time to work out, and that day was no different. As I was lifting weights, I caught a glimpse of my coworker approaching through the mirror. She was smiling.

Immediately, I thought, **I hope this conversation won't be long: I need to finish my workout**. But I shifted my mindset and prepared to listen.

She walked up to me and said, "Ron, you probably don't know what's going on with me, but my father is in the hospital, and I've been praying."

I listened as she continued.

"When you smiled at me this morning, your smile was so powerful: it spoke louder than any words could have, and at that moment, God told me everything would be okay."

Then she turned and walked away, leaving me standing there, reflecting.

That moment **changed me**. It reminded me that sometimes, all a person needs is a small gesture: **a kind word, a simple hello, a reminder that they're not alone.** We get so caught up in our own world that we forget to check on the people around us. When was the last time you reached out to someone just to see how they were doing? When was the last time someone did that for you?

For me, my circle is small, and to be honest, I often find myself checking on others more than they check on me. But I've learned that when no one else is around, **God is always there.** When I need to talk, He listens. When I'm struggling, He understands. The Bible tells us to **cast all our cares on Him because He cares for us (1 Peter 5:7).** No matter how alone you feel, God sees you.

And sometimes, God will use a stranger to encourage you.

The Bible says we should be careful how we treat people because we may be **entertaining angels without knowing it (Hebrews 13:2).** Every encounter we have is an opportunity to love, to give, to reflect the heart of God.

Think about this: **God gave us everything**. He gave us **His Son**, offering salvation to a world that didn't deserve it. He gave us **grace**, freely pouring out mercy even when we fail. He gave us **purpose**, a plan for our lives that is greater than we can imagine. His Spirit guides us, His love sustains us, and every single morning, His mercies are new **(Lamentations 3:22-23)**.

And yet, some people will never give anything back.

They won't use the gifts He placed inside them. They won't share their testimony. They won't serve, they won't love, they won't forgive. **They live their lives withholding what God freely gave them.**

Imagine getting a zero percent return on your investment.

That's what some people give to God. **Nothing.**

But here's the good news: **God still gives.**

- Even when we forget Him.
- Even when we ignore Him.
- Even when we take Him for granted.

That's love.

Today, I challenge you to reflect on all that God has poured into your life. **What gifts, talents, and opportunities has He given you? Are you using them to serve others and glorify**

Him, or are you holding back? God's love is an investment in you, and He is calling you to invest that love into the world. Every small act of kindness, every moment you share His grace, can make a powerful difference.

God has placed you exactly where you are for a reason. You may not always see the return, but know this: your obedience to Him will never be in vain.

Don't wait for the perfect moment or for everything to fall into place. The time is now. Step forward in faith, trusting that God will equip you for every good work. The world is waiting for your smile, your heart, your obedience. Will you answer His call and invest in others, just as God has invested in you?

Pray with me

Lord,

Thank You for being patient with me, for calling me even when I ignored You. Forgive me for the times I've placed everything else above You. Today, I choose to answer Your call. I surrender my plans for Yours. I give You my gifts, my time, my heart, because You gave everything for me. Help me to love as You love, to give as You give, and to never take Your presence for granted. I trust You, and I say yes to all You have for me.

In Jesus' name,
Amen.

Day 48

Answer the Call

It's important to have good people in your corner. Not a crowd, not a thousand acquaintances, but true friends: the kind who make you better, who push you, challenge you, and refuse to let you settle for less than God's best. These are the people who won't let you sit in self-pity, who don't agree with everything you say just to keep the peace. They hold you accountable, speak truth in love, and show up when it matters most. I can name the few people in my life who fit that description: friends who would drop everything, no questions asked. And they know exactly who they are.

But let me ask you: **Can you name two people right now who would do the same for you?** If you called them at 3 a.m., would they answer? If you needed them in another state, another country, would they get on a plane? Now, let's flip that. **Would you do the same for them?**

Now, let's take this deeper. **How many times has Jesus called you, and you answered?** Be honest. For me, the answer wasn't always yes. There were times I ignored His voice, put Him on hold, or silenced Him altogether. Yet, He kept calling. I was quick to answer calls from the wrong people: people who meant harm, who led me further from where God wanted me to be. Why is it so easy to entertain distractions, yet so hard to surrender to the One who gave everything for us?

I used to run from God like Jonah, but thankfully, He didn't have to send a great fish to swallow me whole. Life itself became my storm. The more I resisted Him, the harder things became. I wanted to be the captain of my own ship, steering my own course. But here's the truth: **God's way is always greater than our own.** He asks us to surrender, not to take something from us, but to give us something far better. The Bible says, *"Faith is being sure of what we hope for and certain of what we do not see"* (**Hebrews 11:1**).

When we try to take control, we limit ourselves. But when we trust God, He does the impossible. When the storm raged around the disciples, Jesus calmed the sea (**Mark 4:39**). When thousands were hungry, He multiplied five loaves and two fish (**Matthew 14:13-21**). If He did it then, **how much more will He do for you when you say yes to His call?**

Right now, Jesus is calling. Calling you out of the pain, the fear, the confusion. Calling you out of that dark place. **Will you answer?** Take a chance on Him. Watch how He transforms your life.

The greatest relationship you will ever have, the only one you can count on 100% of the time, is with God. Don't take my word for it: **try Him**. My life changed the moment I surrendered. Do I have it all together? No. But I've never known a love greater than His. Whatever you're facing, **God is the answer. Answer the call.**

Pray with me

Heavenly Father,

I come before You with an open heart. I surrender my plans, my fears, my need for control. Forgive me for the times I ignored Your voice, for the moments I chose my way over Yours. Lord, I say yes to You today. Help me to trust You fully, to follow where You lead, and to embrace the life You have prepared for me. Thank You for Your unending grace and love.

In Jesus' name,
Amen.

Day 49

Forgiven, Yet Growing

Have you ever thought about how your words, thoughts, or actions might have hurt someone; even when you never meant to? Sometimes, we move forward, confident that we've been forgiven and redeemed, but then God stops us in our tracks to remind us: **We are not innocent of everything.**

Maybe you spoke out of frustration. Maybe you acted without realizing how it affected someone else. Maybe someone is still carrying pain from something you've long forgotten. Some people may never forgive you. Some may try to tarnish your name. But here's the truth: **it's not your job to control how others respond.**

What is up to you is this: **Are you willing to let God show you where you still need His grace?**

I had to take a hard look in the mirror recently. I wanted to believe I had outgrown my past mistakes: that I was no longer the person who hurt others, whether intentionally or unintentionally. But then God reminded me: **Just because you've** changed doesn't mean you're innocent. The Apostle Paul said it best:

"My conscience is clear, but that does not make me innocent." (1 Corinthians 4:4)

That truth hit me. Hard. I realized that even though I wasn't walking in the same mistakes as before, I had still left behind wounds. People I had hurt: some knowingly, some without realizing it. And some wounds don't heal just because we've moved on.

One of the hardest lessons in forgiveness is learning to forgive yourself for the things you cannot fix. Every day, I ask God to cleanse my heart of anything I've done; whether I know about it or not: that doesn't honor Him. It's humbling. It's necessary.

During my prayer time, God reminded me that forgiveness isn't just about saying, "I'm sorry." It's about being **accountable**. It's about looking inward and letting Him prune away the pride, guilt, or shame that keep us from true healing.

That's when He put this question on my heart:

What if, instead of focusing on how others have hurt you, you let Me show you where you need to grow?

Wow. That was a wake-up call.

See, we spend so much time dwelling on the wounds inflicted by others, but how often do we ask God to reveal where we've left scars on someone else?

Jesus didn't say, "**Only forgive the ones who deserve it.**" He said: "**Love your enemies and pray for those who persecute you**" (Matthew 5:44). Even as believers, we can be the ones causing pain, sometimes without realizing it. That's why humility is crucial.

Peter once asked Jesus, *"How many times should I forgive my brother who sins against me? Seven times?"* Jesus replied: *"Not seven times, but seventy-seven times."* (Matthew 18:21-22)

Forgiveness is not a one-time event, it's something we must do over and over. Not just for others, but for ourselves. Maybe you've made peace with your past, but someone else is still carrying the pain. Maybe you've forgiven yourself, but the enemy keeps whispering that you're unworthy. Maybe you're waiting for someone to apologize to you, and it may never happen.

Here's the truth: Holding onto pain; whether it's guilt, resentment, or anger, only slows you down. That's why God calls us to let go. Not for them. For you.

Sometimes, God sits us down for a serious heart-to-heart. He pulls out the areas in our lives that need correction, conviction, and cleansing. And it's uncomfortable.

"For the word of God is alive and active, sharper than any double-edged sword; it penetrates even to dividing soul and spirit, joints and marrow; it judges the thoughts and attitudes of the heart." (Hebrews 4:12)

God's process of refining us is like surgery: it's painful, but it's life-giving. Over time, we heal, we grow, and we reflect more of His glory. But healing requires surrender. If you're still holding onto something: a grudge, guilt, shame, it's time to release it. If you've hurt someone, ask for forgiveness. And if you've been hurt? Forgive, even if they never apologize.

Jesus asked: ***"Why do you look at the speck of sawdust in your brother's eye and pay no attention to the plank in your own eye?"*** (Matthew 7:3)

We're all a work in progress. None of us are without fault. And yet, God's grace is still big enough to cover everything.

God didn't just come for **you**: He came to **save the world**. And as He calls you higher, He will ask you to leave things behind: resentment, guilt, shame, pride. Anything that keeps you stuck.

If He's pressing on your heart to make things right, don't ignore His voice. Maybe it's reaching out to someone you've hurt, offering forgiveness to someone who wronged you, or surrendering your own pain to Him. Whatever it is, let go of what's weighing you down so you can walk fully in His will.

God is calling you to reflect His love, His mercy, and His grace to a world in desperate need of Him.

Pray with me

Heavenly Father,

I come before You with a humble heart. Forgive me for anything I've done; whether I realize it or not: that has hurt You or others. Teach me to forgive as You have forgiven me. Help me let go of what is weighing me down so I can walk fully in Your will. Thank You for Your grace, mercy, and love. May my life reflect You in all things.

In Jesus' name,
Amen.

Day 50

Are You Your Brother or Sister's Keeper?

This isn't just a question; it's a life-changing call. It's an invitation to reflect on how we live and to follow the example of the greatest keeper of all: **Jesus Christ**.

In **Genesis 4:9**, God asked Cain, *"Where is your brother Abel?"* Cain's cold reply was, *"Am I my brother's keeper?"* He was rejecting responsibility, even after committing the unthinkable act of taking his brother's life. But God's Word teaches us the opposite. We are called to care for others, to love them deeply, and to support each other (**Galatians 6:2**).

So let me ask you again: Are you your brother or sister's keeper?

When was the last time you reached out to someone who needed encouragement? When was the last time you listened: really listened, to someone in pain without interrupting or trying to solve their problems? Have you let busyness, pride, or even indifference stop you from showing love to the people God has placed in your life?

I'll be honest with you: this question has challenged me deeply.

Before my brother's life was tragically cut short, we had talked about reconnecting and making up for lost time. But that time never came. When I saw him lying in that casket, the regret hit me hard. None of us are promised tomorrow. We only have **today**: this moment, to make things right.

Is there someone in your life you've been avoiding because of pride, bitterness, or unresolved conflict? Maybe you're waiting for them to make the first move. If that's you, stop and pray. Ask God to help you. Whatever it is, it can be healed. Jesus came to reconcile us to God and to one another. Who are we to withhold forgiveness and grace when He has freely given it to us?

Jesus is our ultimate example. He didn't just talk about love, He lived it. He came to serve, to heal, and to save us while we were still lost, broken, and far from Him **(Romans 5:8)**. Even as He hung on the cross, He prayed for the very people who mocked and crucified Him: *"Father, forgive them, for they know not what they do"* **(Luke 23:34)**. That is love in its purest form: sacrificial, unconditional, and redemptive.

For those of you reading this who may not yet follow Christ, let me tell you this: Jesus lived the life we could never live: a life of perfect love and obedience, and then He died the death we deserved so that we could be free. He didn't come to condemn you but to save you. He sees your struggles, your questions, and your pain, and He invites you to bring it all to Him.

In **Matthew 11:28-30**, Jesus says: *"Come to me, all you who are weary and burdened, and I will give you rest. Take my yoke upon you and learn from me, for I am gentle and* *humble in heart, and you will find rest for your souls. For my yoke is easy and my burden is light."*

You don't have to face life's challenges on your own. Jesus is calling you to trust Him and let Him transform your heart.

For those who already follow Him, ask yourself: Does your life reflect His love? Are you actively caring for others, or have you allowed distractions to silence your compassion?

Take this challenge: Think of someone you've been avoiding, someone who needs your forgiveness or encouragement. Maybe it's a family member, a friend, or even a stranger. Pray for them and reach out. You might think you're helping them, but God could use that moment to change you.

Last night, I texted a family member I hadn't spoken to in years. I asked for forgiveness for not being present in their life. They responded with unexpected grace: **"There's no need for forgiveness. Let's not live in the past. Let's live in the now."** In that moment, I realized something profound: I thought I was offering help, but in reality, she was the one setting me free.

The Bible reminds us in **1 John 4:20**: *"Whoever claims to love God yet hates a brother or sister is a liar. For whoever does not love their brother and sister, whom they have seen, cannot love God, whom they have not seen."*

God created us for relationships: with Him and with each other. But we cannot truly love others without first receiving His love. If you've never made the decision to follow Christ, let today be the day. He's waiting for you with open arms.

For those of us who already know Him, let's live as He lived. Let's be the hands and feet of Jesus, showing love to the broken, the hurting, and the forgotten. Let's remember that this life is not about us but about glorifying God and reflecting His love to the world.

The world desperately needs light. And Jesus said in **Matthew 5:14**, *"You are the light of the world."* Will you let His light shine through you? **Will you step out in faith and become your brother or sister's keeper?**

Pray with me

Lord Jesus,

Thank You for loving me even when I was far from You. I confess that I've fallen short in showing love to others. Forgive me, Lord, and fill me with Your love and compassion. Help me to follow Your example, to reach out to those in need, and to forgive those who have hurt me. I surrender my life to You. Teach me to walk in Your ways and to be a light in this dark world. Thank You for Your sacrifice, for Your grace, and for the hope You give.

**In Jesus' name,
Amen.**

Day 51

Let It Go

Listen loud and clear: **Let it go!** Whatever is stopping you from living the life God has planned for you, it's time to release it. You've been carrying this weight far too long. **Today** is the day to break free and let it go.

Maybe it's unforgiveness. Maybe you're being too hard on yourself because your life isn't where you thought it would be. Maybe people have let you down, or you're carrying something so heavy it consumes every waking moment. Perhaps your mind is restless, filled with unquiet thoughts, and the people you relied on disappeared when you needed them most. Maybe you're silently punishing someone for something that isn't even true. Whatever it is, it's time to let it go.

Holding on to things that have held you back has taken up too much space in your heart and life. God is asking you to **let them go** and make room for His peace and plan for you.

Before my father passed away, he often repeated these words to me: **"Live your life. Don't live anyone else's life, and don't let anyone else live yours."** At the time, I nodded and said,

"Okay, Pop." But I didn't fully understand the depth of his wisdom until later.

For so long, I was living a false reality: trying to please people, to gain acceptance, and in doing so, I erased parts of my God-given identity. I was trying to fit into a mold that wasn't mine. Sound familiar?

Too often, we mimic the lives of others: people on social media, celebrities, coworkers, or even friends. We tell ourselves that if we could just be more like them, life would make sense. But when God created you, He broke the mold. You weren't meant to be like anyone else. *You are fearfully and wonderfully made* **(Psalm 139:14)**.

It's not wrong to admire greatness in others. But the challenge arises when we trade our authenticity for a counterfeit version of someone else. **God created you with a unique and divine purpose,** and He gave you gifts meant for His glory, not to be buried, compared, or diminished.

Jesus teaches us in the Parable of the Talents **(Matthew 25:14-30)** that we are called to use the gifts entrusted to us, not hide them out of fear. If you don't know what your gift is, ask God. He's been waiting for you to seek Him. **Jeremiah 29:13** reminds us: *"You will seek Me and find Me when you seek Me with all your heart."*

Let me tell you this: You are powerful beyond measure. You are not mediocre. Stop surrounding yourself with people who merely tolerate you instead of celebrating you. God created you to be a light in this world **(Matthew 5:14-16)**. Shine boldly, because your light not only glorifies God but also frees others to shine alongside you.

Yes, some people will envy your success. Others may criticize or attempt to dim your light. But that's not your burden to carry. Remember, their insecurity isn't your responsibility. Continue to shine, because God didn't place His light in you for it to be hidden. *"Let your light shine before others, that they may see your good deeds and glorify your Father in heaven"* **(Matthew 5:16)**.

Whatever gift God has given you, use it for His glory. Don't seek to build riches for yourself without a heart to serve others, because true joy doesn't come from material wealth, it comes from fulfilling your purpose in Christ. Jesus Himself said, *"The Son of Man did not come to be served, but to serve"* **(Matthew 20:28)**. He modeled a life of sacrifice, humility, and love for others.

So I challenge you today: Pray that God meets you where you are and reveals just how amazing you are in His eyes. Whether your dream is to open a business, become an artist, or lead others to Christ, nothing can stop you, except you. The only limitations are the ones you place on yourself.

I am living proof of this truth. God placed the gift of writing in me, and I use it to glorify Him. Whatever your gift is, embrace it. Use it to uplift, encourage, and serve others. Let your life be a reflection of God's goodness, grace, and purpose.

When God sent Jesus, He gave us His best. Will you give Him yours?

If you're ready to let go of what's holding you back.

Let it go. Step into the life God has prepared for you. Your breakthrough is waiting. You've got this, and God's got you.

Pray with me

Heavenly Father,

Thank You for creating me with purpose and for loving me unconditionally. I ask You to help me release every burden, every fear, and every distraction that's keeping me from living the life You designed for me. Reveal the gifts You've placed within me and guide me as I use them to glorify You. Teach me to let my light shine boldly and to trust that Your plan for my life is good. I surrender my heart to You today.

In Jesus' name,
Amen.

Day 52

When God Shifts Your Life

Have you ever heard the saying, **"It's lonely at the top"?** On the surface, it might seem like something only the successful or powerful experience. But its meaning runs much deeper; especially when applied to your spiritual journey.

From a worldly perspective, "lonely at the top" means that when someone achieves a high level of success, they often feel isolated. People treat them differently, making genuine relationships hard to maintain.

But from a **spiritual perspective,** this phrase takes on new meaning. When God begins to shift your life, calling you into a deeper relationship with Him, you may feel isolated too. Some relationships, habits, or environments will fall off, and you might feel like no one understands. This is not a punishment: it's a process. God is pruning you, preparing you, and positioning you for where He's taking you.

Think about a tree in the fall. As the season changes, the tree loses its leaves. But this doesn't mean the tree is dying. It's simply preparing for the growth that will come in spring.

In the same way, when God calls you higher, He removes what no longer serves His purpose for your life. It could be a relationship, a job, or even a mindset. These things served you for a season, but they can't go where God is taking you.

This process can be painful. You might feel lonely or even blame yourself for the changes happening around you. But know this: it's not your fault. God is simply shaking the tree, removing what doesn't belong, so He can bring new blessings in their place.

As **Ecclesiastes 3:1** reminds us, *"There is a time for everything, and a season for every activity under the heavens."* When one season ends, God is preparing you for the next.

There was a time in my life when I felt like a barren tree. It seemed like everyone who once stood by me had walked away. I felt alone, misunderstood, and unsure of what God was doing. Then, one day, my sister called and said words that forever changed my perspective:

"Be still and know that God is God." (Psalm 46:10)

At that moment, I realized that my loneliness wasn't punishment, it was preparation. God wanted my attention. He wanted me to rely on Him completely, without distractions. And though it hurt, I began to understand that losing people, places, or things didn't mean I was losing God.

When God calls you higher, some people won't be able to come with you. Not everyone can understand the transformation God is doing in your life. Some will misunderstand you. Others will judge you. And yes, some will walk away.

Jesus experienced this too. On the cross, He was abandoned by many who once followed Him. Yet, even in His suffering, He prayed for those responsible for His crucifixion, saying, *"Father, forgive them, for they do not know what they are doing"* **(Luke 23:34)**. Jesus demonstrated His love and mercy, even for those who rejected and betrayed Him.

Take heart in knowing that when people walk away, God never does. As **Deuteronomy 31:8** assures us, *"The Lord Himself goes before you and will be with you; He will never leave you nor forsake you."*

Throughout Scripture, we see examples of God isolating His chosen people to prepare them for their purpose. Moses spent 40 years in the desert before leading Israel out of Egypt. David fled to the wilderness before becoming king. Even Jesus often withdrew to lonely places to pray.

Maybe that's where you are now. If so, know that God hasn't abandoned you. He's setting you apart for something greater. He's aligning your life with His will and preparing you to fulfill your calling.

As **Isaiah 43:19** says, *"See, I am doing a new thing! Now it springs up; do you not perceive it? I am making a way in the wilderness and streams in the wasteland."*

When people walk out of your life, and trust me they will, don't chase after them. Instead, chase after God. Trust that He is working all things together for your good **(Romans 8:28)**. Pray for those who misunderstand you, forgive those who hurt you, and stay focused on the path God has laid before you.

Take time to seek Him in prayer, worship, and His Word. Ask Him to reveal what He's doing in this season of your life. And remember: when you draw closer to God, He will draw closer to you (**James 4:8**).

Remember, when God shifts your life, it's not to harm you—it's to transform you. He's not just taking things away; He's making room for new blessings, new opportunities, and a deeper relationship with Him.

You're not alone in this journey. Trust the process. Trust God. And know that His plans for you are always good.

Pray with me

Heavenly Father,

Thank You for always being with me, even when I feel alone. Help me to trust Your plan, even when I don't understand it. I surrender the people, places, and things You are removing from my life, and I trust that You are making room for something greater. Strengthen me in this season of isolation, and remind me that You are my refuge and my strength. Teach me to forgive those who have walked away and to focus on the path You have set before me. Lord, I put my hope in You and trust that You are working all things for my good.

In Jesus' name,
Amen.

Day 53

Worship Changes Everything

I remember sitting in church, minding my own business, when a woman of God preaching on stage looked out into the crowd and said, **"You in the green and white shirt, stand up."**

My eyes moved quickly around the room, trying to figure out who she was talking to. Surely, it couldn't be me. But as I scanned the audience, I felt her eyes lock onto me. Then I looked down and realized: **I was wearing a green and white shirt.**

The room seemed to blur as my heart raced. "No way she's talking to me," I thought, shifting in my seat, hoping to blend into the crowd. But then she called out again, louder this time. **"Yes, you. I'm talking to you."**

I froze. No part of me wanted to stand up in front of a room full of strangers. Before I could decide, an older gentleman next to me gently pulled me to my feet. Heart pounding, I stood there, unsure of what would happen next.

She looked me straight in the eyes and said, "I have a word for you. God told me someone is trying to steal your creativity. But He wants you to worship Him and Him alone. When life gets tough, He wants you to worship Him. When you don't know which direction to walk, He wants you to worship Him. And when you begin to worship Him, your blessings will chase you down because your obedience to Him is greater than any sacrifice."

I didn't fully grasp the meaning of her words at the time. But now, years later, I see how true they are. That moment in church wasn't just about me, it was about all of us who let fear hold us back from answering God's call.

So let me ask you: What or who are you chasing more than God? Is it a career? A dream? A relationship? Money? Success?

We often say we're waiting on God, but the truth is: He's already done His part. The question is, are you doing yours? The Bible reminds us in **James 2:17** that *"faith by itself, if it is not accompanied by action, is dead."*

When God calls you, it won't always be easy. You might feel alone. You might face discouragement, heartache, or fear. But sometimes, God allows these challenges to strip away what doesn't belong and replace it with the truth of His Word. Just like I could've ignored that woman's call and stayed in my seat, you have a choice. Will you sit back, or will you stand up in faith?

Here's the truth: When you put God first, everything else falls into place. Jesus said in **Matthew 6:33**, *"Seek first the king-*

dom of God and His righteousness, and all these things will be added to you."

Proverbs 3:5-6 reminds us, "*Trust in the Lord with all your heart and lean not on your own understanding; in all your ways submit to Him, and He will make your paths straight."*

The blessings you're chasing will begin to chase you down when your life aligns with Him. It's not about what you're doing for yourself; it's about what you're doing for His glory.

So today, I challenge you to ask yourself: What is holding you back from chasing God? Are you prioritizing temporary things over eternal ones? Lay it all down at His feet. Stop running after the things of this world and start running after the One who created it.

Now is the time to stand up in faith. The moment is now. Worship God with your whole heart, and watch Him transform your life in ways you never imagined. God isn't asking for perfection: He's asking for your heart. Stand up, step out, and trust Him to lead the way.

Pray with me

Heavenly Father,

Thank You for loving me even when I've been chasing after everything but You. I surrender my fears, my plans, and my desires to You right now. Help me to let go of the things I've been holding onto so tightly; things that aren't from You. Teach me to worship You in spirit and truth, no matter what I'm facing.

Reveal to me the areas where I've been holding back, and give me the courage to step out in faith. Remind me that obedience to You is worth more than anything I could ever give up. Fill me with Your peace and purpose, and help me to trust that Your plans for me are good.

I choose today to seek You first. Let everything I do bring You glory. Thank You for being my constant source of strength and my guide.

In Jesus' name,
Amen.

Day 54

When Love Speaks in Silence

A few weeks ago, I traveled to Boston to visit my family, and it changed me. I didn't know what to expect, but the idea of seeing them in person after so long made me both excited and a little nervous. As I drove from the airport in a rental car, questions raced through my mind: **How would my mom react when she saw me? Would she cry? Would I cry? Would this moment live up to everything I'd hoped for?** With every mile, my excitement kept building.

When I arrived at my sister's house and rang the doorbell, she was the first to greet me. My sister: a true warrior in both mind and spirit, wrapped me in a **hug that felt like home**. Through her tears, she whispered, "I'm so happy you're here." Her words echoed in my heart as she led me upstairs to see my mom.

Standing at the doorway of my mom's room, time seemed to slow. There she was, the woman who raised five children on her own, the hero of my life. She looked up at me with a smile that gave off pure love. Though she had grown frailer since my last visit, she was still the strong, selfless woman who had always put her family first. We embraced, and in that moment,

I was reminded of all the sacrifices she made to ensure we had a better life.

The days I spent in Boston were a **gift**. My sister and I grew closer, and I was reminded of the importance of family and faith. Through it all, one truth stood out: time waits for no one. Life is fleeting, and every moment is an opportunity to honor God, love others, and walk in the purpose He's called us to.

My mother always taught me two important lessons: to put God first, and to chase my dreams with all my heart. *"Seek first His kingdom and His righteousness, and all these things will be given to you as well"* (Matthew 6:33). Her words remain a guiding light in my life, a reminder that everything we do should bring glory to God.

So, let me ask you: What's holding you back from living the life God has called you to? Is it fear? Doubt? The opinions of others? Are you waiting for the perfect moment? Let me tell you: there's no such thing as the **"perfect moment."** The time to step out in faith is now.

Too often, we carry burdens God never intended for us to bear. We seek approval from people who may never understand our purpose. Some of us are weighed down by unforgiveness, holding onto past hurts and letting bitterness take away our peace and happiness. Yet, God calls us to let go of these things and trust Him to guide us. *"Come to me, all who are weary and burdened, and I will give you rest"* (Matthew 11:28).

Have you ever felt discouraged because the people you thought would support you didn't? Maybe you shared your dreams, only to be met with doubt or silence. But remember, not everyone is meant to walk with you on the journey God has planned for you. Even Jesus warned, **"Behold, I am sending you out as sheep among wolves"** **(Matthew 10:16)**. Guard your heart and your dreams. Share them with God, who will lead you according to His perfect plan.

When you start seeing your life through God's eyes, everything changes. It's time to rise above the negativity and walk boldly in faith. *Dr. Martin Luther King Jr.* once said, *"If you can't fly, then run. If you can't run, then walk. If you can't walk, then crawl. But whatever you do, you have to keep moving forward."* And he was right. No matter your circumstances, keep pressing on with the strength God gives you.

The truth is, the only thing standing between you and the life God has for you is your willingness to say **"yes"** to Him. Stop waiting for others to approve of you. Stop allowing fear, failure, or the heaviness of your past to hold you back. Instead, release it all to God and step boldly into His promises.

Ask yourself: What dream has God placed on your heart? What step of faith have you been avoiding? Take one step: no matter how small, toward that dream today. Whether it's praying, writing it down, or simply saying **"yes"** to God, trust that with every step forward, He is walking with you. The time is now. Don't wait. God's promises are waiting for you to step into them.

Pray with me

Lord,

I come to You with an open heart, ready to let go of everything holding me back. I surrender my fears, my doubts, my plans, and my past to You. I give You control over my life, trusting that Your ways are better than mine.

Lord, I ask You to lead me. Shape me into who You've created me to be. I surrender my dreams and trust You to guide me toward the purpose You have for me. Help me to let go of trying to do it all on my own and lean on Your strength, Your love, and Your wisdom.

Thank You for loving me, even when I fall short. I am Yours, Lord: fully and completely.

In Jesus' name,
Amen.

Day 55

The Power to Choose Light

What if I told you that you hold the power to change your life right now? You can step into a life of purpose, open the gifts within you, and walk boldly into the future you've been dreaming of. The choice is yours. But here's the catch: it's not just about the choices you make, it's also about the ones you don't make.

Let me share a story: a real-life example about how light can shine even in the darkest times.

Most people who know me might assume I've always been this way: the kind of guy who greets everyone with a smile and would give away the shirt off his back. Well, let me tell you, that hasn't always been the case. Truth be told, I probably wouldn't give you the shirt off my back today, **but I'd happily buy you one!** I grew up in Boston, Massachusetts, in a neighborhood where poverty and crime were the norm. By all accounts, my surroundings were pure darkness. Yet even in that darkness, a light was always there, waiting to guide me.

At an early age, my mother signed me and my siblings up at the local Boys and Girls Club to keep us off the streets. That decision changed my life. At the club, I saw opportunities I never knew existed. It felt like the brightest star in the sky was shining on me, showing me there was more to life than the darkness surrounding me. It was there that I learned life's most valuable lessons, lessons that shaped the man I am today. Even when the streets around me were dark, God's light was always present, guiding me forward, just as He's guiding you.

Sure, I could've taken the wrong path. Many of my friends did. But **Matthew 7:13–14** reminds us there are two roads: one wide and easy, leading to destruction, and one narrow and difficult, leading to life. **We each have a choice.**

Later in life, after college, I found myself hanging out with a group of tough guys who weren't impressed by my education. I thought I could balance it all: keep one foot on the narrow path while dabbling in the wide road. But those choices came with consequences. I found myself on a path that led closer to darkness. Yet, even in those moments, there was still light inside me: a light God had placed there, patiently waiting to guide me back.

One day, when I was at my lowest, God's light broke through the darkness in my life. It was as if scales fell from my eyes, and I could see clearly for the first time. From that moment on, I chose to turn away from darkness and toward the light.

Here's what I've learned: light and darkness coexist. Choosing the light doesn't mean life gets easier. In fact, the brighter your light shines, the more the darkness notices. **But no matter how**

hard it tries, darkness cannot overcome the light God has placed within you.

The world will tempt you with quick fixes; temporary pleasures and promises of success. But what do those things cost you? With God, the blessings are abundant and eternal. The choice is yours: light or darkness.

Romans 8:37 reminds us, *"In all these things we are more than conquerors through Him who loved us."* With God, you've already won.

Some of us are stuck. We're in relationships we know we shouldn't be in. We're hanging out with people who pull us away from God. We're staying in jobs God told us to leave long ago. Why are you still there? Why are you still stuck? Fear is often the answer. But **Joshua 1:9** tells us, *"Be strong and courageous. Do not be afraid; do not be discouraged, for the Lord your God will be with you wherever you go."*

What if the life you've been praying for is on the other side of that fear?

So, what will **you** choose? **Light or darkness?** God's truth or the world's distractions? Today, you can decide to walk in the light and embrace the purpose God has prepared for you.

Darkness may try to fight you, but it cannot win. Look in the mirror and remind yourself: **"Happiness is within me. Joy is within me. Greatness is within me, because God is within me."**

Take a moment to reflect. **What's holding you back from stepping into the light?** What's one decision you can make today to move closer to the life God has for you?

Share this message with someone who needs to hear it. You never know how God can use a simple act to change someone's life. And as you move forward, remember: you've got this, because God's got you.

Pray with me

Heavenly Father,

Thank You for shining Your light into my life. When I face choices, remind me of the greatness You've placed within me and guide me to walk boldly in Your purpose. Help me trust Your plan over the distractions of this world. Awaken my spirit to Your truth and surround me with Your peace and favor.

In Jesus' name,
Amen.

Day 56

Who Are You Living For?

Have you ever stopped to think about how much of your identity has been shaped by others? From the moment we're born, we absorb the thoughts, beliefs, and expectations of those around us. But too often, these voices don't reflect who we truly are. Instead, they lead us to doubt ourselves and search for approval from others, causing us to lose touch with the person God created us to be.

Does that sound familiar? It does to me.

For years, I lived behind a mask. I'm not afraid to admit it. After hearing countless times that I wasn't good enough, I hid. I was too afraid to let people see the real me. I worried they wouldn't accept me, so I tried to become what I thought they wanted. But deep down, I felt lost. My thoughts, decisions, and dreams weren't my own: **they were shaped by others**.

In my book *Secrets End*, the main character faces a similar struggle. He seems to have it all: success, wealth, and admiration. But inside, he's empty because he's living a life built on other people's expectations. His breakthrough comes when he's faced with a life-changing decision. He chooses to take off the mask, defy the world's opinions, and live a life true to himself.

That story mirrors a choice we all face: Will we keep living for others, or will we live for God?

The battle for our identity begins in our minds. **Romans 12:2** reminds us: ***"Do not conform to the pattern of this world, but be transformed by the renewing of your mind."***

When we let the world, or even well-meaning people control our thoughts, we lose touch with who God created us to be. It's like handing someone else the pen and letting them write your story.

But here's the **good news**: God wants to help you take back your thoughts. He wants you to see yourself as He does: worthy, loved, and full of potential.

Living authentically takes courage. It's about standing firm in who you are, even when others don't understand or try to move you in a different direction. Too often, we hide our true selves, either to fit in or because we're afraid of judgment. We search for validation, measuring our worth by the opinions of others, yet deep down, we know we're meant for more.

The world is filled with imitation. People try to be someone they're not, and the pressure to conform; whether from social media, family, or friends, can be overwhelming. But here's the truth: **God made you one of a kind.** There's no one else on this earth like you. **When He made you, He tied destiny to your life.**

You can admire the courage of David as he faced Goliath or the patience of Noah as he built the ark, but God didn't create you to copy their journeys. **Psalm 139:14** reminds us: *"I praise You because I am fearfully and wonderfully made."* You were made with purpose, and you are already enough. Trusting in this truth allows you to let go of the need for others' approval, empowering you to live boldly and authentically.

Many of us spend our lives waiting: waiting for approval, success, or relationships to complete us. Yet, the blessings we seek are already within reach. **They begin with seeking God.** When you seek Him, you'll discover your true self. He leads you to a life filled with peace, purpose, and joy: a life that's uniquely yours.

John 10:10 assures us: *"I have come that they may have life, and have it to the full."* True fulfillment resides in living as the person God created you to be.

Living authentically begins with God. Stop waiting for the perfect moment to take off the mask. **The perfect moment is now.** Seek Him, trust Him, and let Him guide you into a life of freedom, purpose, and joy.

Remember this: **there is no one and nothing on earth greater than God.** His love for you is unmatched, His plans for you are perfect, and His power to transform your life is limitless.

Your story isn't over. With God, it's just beginning.

Pray with me

Heavenly Father,

I come to You with an open heart. For too long, I've allowed the world to shape my thoughts and identity. I've worn masks and lived for others' approval instead of seeking Yours. Forgive me, Lord, and help me to see myself through Your eyes. Teach me to trust in Your plan for my life and to walk in the purpose You've created for me. Thank You for loving me unconditionally and for guiding me toward the person You designed me to be.

In Jesus' name,
Amen.

Day 57

The Mind: Your Greatest Ally or Your Worst Enemy

The mind is one of the most powerful tools we have. It shapes our reality, influences our actions, and impacts our well-being. It gives life to our dreams, solve problems, and guide us though life's challenges. But if you don't keep it in check, it can turn against you. It can transform doubts into fears, build unnecessary worries, and steer us toward self-sabotage. It can twist the truth, making lies feel real, and cause misunderstandings that damage relationships.

Let's be real: haven't we all been there?

Have you ever assumed something about someone that turned out to be completely false? I remember a time when I was working out and noticed a man staring in my direction. My immediate thought was, **What's his problem?** I let that thought spiral, assuming the worst. Finally, I confronted him, only to find out he wasn't even looking at me, he was lost in his own thoughts, dealing with his own struggles. That experience **humbled me**. It reminded me how easily our minds can twist reality when we don't check our thoughts against the truth.

This isn't a new problem, it's been around since the beginning of time.

Think about Adam and Eve. The serpent didn't physically force Eve to eat the forbidden fruit. He simply planted a seed of doubt in her mind, convincing her that God was withholding something good. She believed the lie, and the rest is history.

The enemy knows the mind is where the real battle happens. If he can mess with your thoughts, he can influence your choices. But here's the good news: you can take back control. You are not a failure. You are not the lies others have told you. You are not the doubts you've believed. You are a child of God, made in His image, and His plan for you is good.

But you have to protect your mind. Be careful who you let influence your thoughts and emotions. Not everyone who speaks into your life is meant to shape it. Some people may plant seeds of doubt, while others bring wisdom and encouragement. Ask God for help to tell the difference.

Proverbs 4:23 reminds us: *"Above all else, guard your heart, for everything you do flows from it."* Your heart and mind are deeply connected. If you let doubt, fear, or negativity grow, it will show in your life. But when you fill your mind with God's truth, your life will flourish.

We need God's help to know what's true and what's a lie. Without it, we risk believing things that lead to anxiety, fear, and unhealthy relationships. **Galatians 1:10** challenges us to examine our motives: *"Am I now trying to win the approval of human beings, or of God? Or am I trying to please people? If*

I were still trying to please people, I would not be a servant of Christ."

Ask yourself: Are you living for what others think, or for what God says? Are you letting anyone and everyone have access to your emotions and thoughts, even when they don't honor God? Not everyone who speaks into your life is meant to shape it. Seek out voices that bring wisdom and encouragement, and always compare what they say to God's Word.

It's never too late to change what's going on in your mind. Stop wasting time believing lies or holding on to unhealthy connections. **Jeremiah 17:7-8** says: **"But blessed is the one who trusts in the Lord, whose confidence is in him. They will be like a tree planted by the water that sends out its roots by the stream. It does not fear when heat comes; its leaves are always green."**

Declare this over your life:

"I am not what the lies say I am. I am a child of God. My mind is renewed, my heart is protected, and my life is rooted in His truth."

Let those words guide you. Be intentional about what you allow into your mind and heart. Trust that God's truth will always lead you to peace and purpose.

Here is a Prayer for Renewing Your Mind.

Pray with me

Heavenly Father,

Thank You for giving me a mind capable of great things. Help me to guard it against lies and negativity. Fill my thoughts with Your truth and guide me with Your wisdom. Teach me to discern what is from You and what is not. I surrender my fears and doubts, trusting that You are in control. Let my life reflect the peace and purpose that come from walking in Your truth.

In Jesus' name,
Amen.

Day 58

Happiness Is Within You

What if everything you've been searching for: happiness, peace, and purpose, has been inside you all along? What if the answers you seek are already within your reach, waiting for you to recognize them?

Too often, we fall into the trap of comparison, looking at someone else's life and measuring our worth against theirs. We convince ourselves that happiness lies in having what they have or being who they are. Add in the weight of negative self-talk, and we end up chasing a version of happiness that was **never** meant for us.

But the truth is, you were made in the image of God. You are a masterpiece, uniquely crafted by the Creator of the universe. What greater joy is there than to be connected to Him?

Let me ask you this: how many times have you told yourself, **"I'll be happy when…"?** When I find the right partner. When I get that promotion. When I lose the weight. But then the moment comes, and happiness still feels out of reach. Why? Because true happiness can't be found in the things we acquire or achieve. **It doesn't come from the world around us, it comes from within.**

As a kid, I thought happiness was unwrapping the perfect Christmas gift. I'd wait all year, hoping for that one toy I just had to have. When I finally got it, the excitement lasted a few days before it joined the forgotten pile in the corner. **Sound familiar?**

The "toys" changed as I grew older: a relationship, a new job, a car, a big goal, but the **pattern stayed the same.** Temporary joy, followed by a lasting emptiness. Then, one day, I realized the truth: happiness doesn't come from what we acquire. **True happiness comes from the love of God and knowing He's already given us everything we need.**

You see, happiness isn't something you find; it's something you choose. It's waking up each day and saying, "I trust You, God. I trust that You've placed joy within me, and I don't need to chase it anywhere else."

Here's the thing: you were made in the image of God. Let that sink in for a moment. The Creator of the universe: the One who made the stars and oceans, **also made you.** What greater joy is there than to be connected to Him, to know you are deeply loved and fully known?

We can look around and compare our lives to others, but where does that leave us? Frustrated, discouraged, stuck in negative self-talk. But that's not who you are. **You are God's creation. You are enough, just as you are.**

God has placed so much potential inside of you: unique dreams, talents, and purpose. You don't have to wait for the perfect moment or someone else's validation. The Creator of heaven and earth already sees you as worthy.

But here's my challenge for you: stop waiting. Stop doubting. Stop telling yourself that you'll step into your purpose someday. The time is now. Happiness is already inside you because God is already inside you.

Jesus reminds us in **John 14:27**, **"Peace I leave with you; my peace I give you. I do not give to you as the world gives. Do not let your hearts be troubled and do not be afraid."** The peace and joy you've been searching for are already yours: they've been gifted to you by Him.

Whatever is holding you back: fear, insecurity, comparison, let it go. The same God who raised Jesus from the dead lives in you. Do you realize how powerful that is? You have greatness within you because He is within you.

Look in the mirror and declare: **"Happiness is within me. Joy is within me. Greatness is within me, because God is within me."**

Now, don't just say it. Believe it. Live it. Let it change how you walk through this world. The time to step into your purpose isn't someday: **it's today**.

Pray with me

Father God,

Thank You for creating me in Your image and filling me with joy and purpose. I surrender my fears and distractions to You, trusting in the greatness You've already placed inside me. Help me to walk boldly, to trust You fully, and to live the life You've called me to live. Thank You for Your peace, Your love, and the constant reminder that You are always with me. I don't lack anything because I have You.

In Jesus' name,
Amen.

Day 59

The Power of Patience

Have you ever wanted something so much that waiting for it felt unbearable? Maybe you've been praying day after day, asking God for an answer, wondering if He's even listening. We've all been there: hoping, waiting, and maybe even doubting.

I'll never forget one of those moments in my life. I was in 10th grade and had just transferred to a new, much bigger school. I was excited about basketball tryouts because I felt ready. I had practiced hard and thought I had what it took to make the team.

On tryout day, I walked into the gym full of confidence, but then I froze. The gym was packed. It looked like every boy in the school had shown up. I found myself staring at the competition, comparing myself to them before we'd even started. Suddenly, my confidence wasn't so strong.

Over the next three days, we pushed ourselves through drills, games, and what felt like endless evaluations. It became clear that most of the spots were already taken by returning players from last year's team. That left only a few openings.

On the final day, the coach gave us the dreaded line: **"If you don't hear from us, good luck next year."** And just like that, the waiting began.

I prayed harder than ever before. "God, please let me make the team." I sat by the phone constantly, hoping for a call or message from the coaches. As the hours stretched into days, my heart sank. By the second day, I hadn't heard anything, and I felt defeated.

Then, as I was heading out of school that afternoon, one of the coaches stopped me at the door. He looked at me and said, "I'll see you at practice tonight."

I was excited! But looking back now, I realize something important: even if I hadn't made the team, God's timing and plan would still have been perfect. That experience taught me a lesson I'll carry for life. Sometimes the answer to our prayers doesn't come when or how we expect. Sometimes it's "no." Other times it's "wait." But no matter what, God's timing is always right.

Proverbs 3:5-6 reminds us, "Trust in the Lord with all your heart and lean not on your own understanding; in all your ways submit to Him, and He will make your paths straight."

The truth is, waiting on God can feel frustrating. We want answers now, and when they don't come, we might try to take matters into our own hands. But when we do, we risk ruining the good plans God has for us.

James 4:3 gives us something to think about: ***"When you ask, you do not receive, because you ask with wrong motives, that you may spend what you get on your pleasures."*** It's a hard truth, but **sometimes we're praying for things that aren't part of God's plan, or we're asking for the wrong reasons.**

God sees what we cannot. He knows when we're ready for something and when we're not. His "no" is often a protection, and His **"wait"** is preparation for something far better.

Isaiah 55:9 puts it beautifully: ***"As the heavens are higher than the earth, so are my ways higher than your ways and my thoughts than your thoughts."***

No matter what decision you're facing or what situation you find yourself in, God's timing is never off. Even when things feel delayed, even when you think you've missed an opportunity, trust that He's right on time.

So what are you waiting for right now? Is it a dream, a relationship, or maybe just peace in your life? Whatever it is, surrender it to God. Trust that His plans are better than yours, and His timing is perfect.

The waiting is never easy, but it's in those moments that we grow. Trusting God doesn't mean you stop hoping; it means you rest in the assurance that He's working for your good. Remember, everything we do should have God at the center. When we truly surrender to His plan, we find peace and purpose that no achievement or relationship could ever provide.

So as you wait, trust that He knows what's best for you. And let today be the day you hand over your dreams and choose faith over frustration. **God's got this: and He's got you.**

Pray with me

Lord,

Let's pray for patience: Lord, I'm coming to You with a heart that struggles to wait. Teach me to trust You, even when I don't understand Your timing. Help me to release my plans and align my desires with Your will. Thank You for seeing the bigger picture and loving me through the waiting.

In Jesus' name,
Amen.

Day 60

Redirecting Your Focus

Let's get real: what do you spend most of your time thinking about? I'm talking about the thoughts that take over your day: the ones that shape how you feel and what you do. Is it a career goal, a relationship, how much money you have in your bank account, or maybe the worry of what tomorrow holds? For some, it's a fear that seems to never go away. We all have something that seems to grab hold of us, don't we?

Here's the truth: what fills your thoughts the most reveals what you truly treasure, and Jesus said it best: ***"For where your treasure is, there your heart will be also"*** (Matthew 6:21).

I'll never forget seventh grade. Like most 12-year-old boys, I thought I had life figured out. But one day, sitting in the school auditorium, my world stopped. A girl: one of the prettiest in school, sang *Whitney Houston's* **The Greatest Love of All,** and her voice was nothing short of angelic. My heart raced, my palms sweated, and in that moment, she became my entire focus. For weeks, I thought about her morning, noon, and night. I even wrote letters I never had the courage to deliver. Looking back, I laugh at how consumed I was. But the lesson remains: we all have something, or someone that captures our hearts. The question is, **does it truly deserve that place?**

Proverbs 4:23 gives a powerful warning: *"Above all else, guard your heart, for everything you do flows from it."* What you allow to capture your heart shapes your life. If it's money, fame, or even a relationship, you might find yourself constantly chasing, yet never satisfied. It's like chasing after something that keeps moving just out of reach. **That's not peace. That's exhaustion.**

Let me make it personal. I'm a dad, and my daughter means the world to me. But what kind of relationship would I have with her if I only spent a couple minutes a day with her? Could I call that a real relationship? No way. But how often do we do the same thing with God; giving Him the leftovers of our time while we pour everything into other things? That's a tough truth to face, isn't it?

Psalm 37:4 says, *"Take delight in the Lord, and He will give you the desires of your heart."* But here's the catch: we can't truly delight in God if we're consumed by everything but Him. It's like saying, **"I love you"** to someone while texting someone else the whole time. You're not really giving yourself.

Sometimes, God wakes us up in the middle of the night, trying to get our attention. But what do we do? We roll over, trying to go back to sleep, unaware that this might be the moment God is trying to speak directly to you. He's not just trying to disrupt your rest: **He's calling you to something more.** Imagine missing out on the chance to connect with the One who created you, simply because you're too distracted by everything else. God doesn't want your spare moments; He wants all of you. So the next time you're woken in the middle of the night, stop and say, **"Here I am, God. I'm listening."** You never know how much you might need to hear from Him.

Here's the hard truth: Anything that takes up more space in your life than God will eventually let you down. Money fades. Careers shift. People disappoint. But God's love and purpose? **They never fail.** When He's the center of your life, you'll find a peace and fulfillment that nothing on earth can give. And once you begin to see everything through that lens, your whole perspective will change.

Let me challenge you: take a moment to reflect on what's truly at the center of your life. What's sitting on the throne of your heart right now? Is it God, or something else?

If it's not God, don't worry. **Change starts with just one step.**

Ask God to help realign your focus on Him. Start by making time for God every day, even if it's just a small step toward a deeper connection. It's not about perfection: it's about being consistent. A real relationship with God begins with a daily commitment, and over time, your heart will align with your devotion.

Your heart will always chase after something. The question is, will it chase after something temporary, or something eternal? **And remember, if you want God to be your top priority, it's not enough just to say it. You've got to show up and live it.**

God wants more than just your time; **He wants your whole heart.** And when you give it to Him, everything else falls into place.

Let today be the day you realign your focus. Let this be the moment you choose Him above all else. You've got this, and I believe in you!

Pray with me

Lord,

Here's a prayer to help you begin: Dear God, thank You for loving me even when my heart is distracted. Show me what has taken Your place in my life, and help me to realign my focus on You. Teach me to delight in You above all else, and fill me with a peace that only You can give.

In Jesus' name,
Amen.

Day 61

Finding Clarity in the Chaos

Have you ever felt like life is one endless, unsolvable puzzle? Imagine this: you're blindfolded, trying to complete a 500-piece puzzle scattered throughout your house. First, you have to find the pieces: stumbling, searching, feeling your way, and then put them together, still blindfolded. To make it worse, there's a ticking clock, reminding you that time is running out. **Doesn't that sound impossible?** Yet for so many of us, that's exactly what life feels like: an overwhelming, chaotic search for answers we can't see or make sense of.

But what if I told you there's another way? What if I told you that the puzzle is already complete, and the **One** who holds the finished picture is ready to guide you every step of the way?

You see, we are the puzzle, and God is the guide. Without Him, we're blindfolded, fumbling in the dark, trying to make sense of a life we were never meant to navigate alone. With Him, the blindfold comes off, and the pieces start to fit together. **The impossible becomes possible.**

Let's keep it real. **Life without God is like trying to drive with a broken GPS. It sends you everywhere except where you need to go.** You think you're making progress, but you're just going in circles, frustrated and lost. I've been there. I thought I could handle life on my own. I chased after relationships, achievements, and material things, thinking they'd fill the emptiness inside me. But no matter how hard I tried, I always ended up feeling stuck, broken, and alone.

There was a point when I hit rock bottom. I remember sitting in my car, overwhelmed by the mess I had made of my life. I felt invisible, like no one saw me or cared. And in that moment of desperation, I cried out, **"God, where are You? Do You even see me?"** And then, something happened. It wasn't a loud voice or a flash of lightning. It was a quiet, steady whisper in my soul: **"I see you. I've always seen you. And I've been waiting for you to let Me in."**

That was the moment everything changed. God didn't just see me; He chose me. He loved me, even in my brokenness. And He's been guiding me ever since.

The Bible says in **Hebrews 11:1**, *"Faith is being sure of what we hope for and certain of what we cannot see."* Faith isn't just believing God exists. It's trusting Him to lead you, even when life doesn't make sense. It's like walking through a storm, knowing that the One holding your hand will get you safely to the other side.

Without God, life's struggles will break you. But with Him, those same struggles become stepping stones to something greater. When you let God guide you, He takes the broken pieces of your life and creates a masterpiece.

When I surrendered to God, He didn't just give me peace: He gave me purpose. He showed me that I wasn't created to simply survive; I was created to succeed. **Psalm 139:14** says, *"I praise you because I am fearfully and wonderfully made; your works are wonderful, I know that full well."* Do you know what that means? It means you're not an accident. You were created with love, intention, and purpose.

God began to use my life in ways I never imagined. Whether through writing, teaching, or simply encouraging others, **He turned my mess into a message**. And you know what? **He can do the same for you.** No matter where you've been or what you've done, God's love is bigger. His grace is greater. All He asks is that you say **yes** to Him.

Look around. We live in a world filled with anxiety, division, and hopelessness. People are searching for meaning, but they're looking in all the wrong places. Politics, money, success: **none of it satisfies.** That's because the answer isn't found in the world; it's found in God. He is the only one who can fill the void in our hearts and bring true peace.

Without Him, life will always feel like that blindfolded puzzle: scattered, frustrating, and impossible to solve. But with Him, everything changes. He brings clarity, strength, and hope. He doesn't just show you the way; He is the way.

So here's my challenge to you: **Stop trying to figure it all out on your own.** Stop carrying the weight of life by yourself. Say **yes** to God today. **It's not about being perfect or having all the answers. It's about surrendering and trusting the One who created you**.

The journey won't always be easy, but I promise you this: With God, it will always be worth it. Your best life starts when you surrender to Him. Don't wait. Say yes to God today. Let Him turn your scattered puzzle into a beautiful masterpiece. You got this!

Pray with me

God,

I can't do this on my own anymore. I need You. Open my eyes, guide my steps, and show me Your purpose for my life. I trust You, and I say yes to Your plan.

In Jesus' name,
Amen.

Day 62

Are You Ready for What You're Asking For?

Have you ever wanted something so deeply that it feels like the waiting might break you? Maybe you've prayed, asking God for a breakthrough: a job, a relationship, healing, or clarity, and yet, nothing seems to be happening. It's easy to wonder, **Why hasn't it come yet? I'm doing everything right. So why not now?**

But let me ask you this: After you've prayed, what do you do?

Do you sit back and wait, assuming God will just drop it into your lap? Do you grow frustrated, complaining about how long it's taking? Or do you start working on yourself, preparing for the blessing you've asked for?

I'll never forget a moment in my life that taught me this lesson in a profound way. I was playing in a championship basketball game, and we lost. After the game, the referee came up to me and said, **"The reason your team lost is because of you."**

I couldn't believe what I was hearing. **Me?** I had led the team in scoring! If it weren't for me, we wouldn't have even made it that far. But instead of brushing off his comment, I asked, "What do you mean?"

He looked me straight in the eye and said, "You're only half a player. You can't dribble with your left hand. If you could, you'd have avoided those traps, and you would've seen more opportunities to help your team."

At first, it stung. But then I realized he was right. Instead of making excuses or ignoring his advice, I made a decision. I was going to fix that weakness. Every single day after that, I practiced dribbling with my left hand: again and again, until it became just as strong as my right.

The next time I stepped on the court, I wasn't just ready; I was unstoppable. Not only did we win the championship that year, but the referee came back to me and said, "Nice job."

Now, think about your own life. **Are you praying for something but not preparing for it?**

The Bible reminds us in **James 2:26**, *"Faith without works is dead."* Faith isn't just about asking, it's about doing. It's about trusting God's timing while actively becoming the person who can handle what you're asking for.

For example, if you're praying for a job, are you developing the skills you'll need for that role? If you're asking for a spouse, are you becoming the kind of partner you'd want to be with? If you're seeking direction, are you spending time in God's Word, listening for His guidance?

Sometimes the delay isn't denial; it's preparation. God, in His infinite wisdom, may withhold what you're asking for because He knows you're not ready: or that receiving it too soon might harm you.

Think back to my basketball game. I thought I was ready, but I wasn't. It took someone challenging me to see what I needed to work on. Similarly, God uses the waiting season to refine us, to shape us into who we need to be.

Here's the truth: **God will never give us something we're not prepared to handle. And when He does bless us, it will come at the right time: when we're spiritually and emotionally mature enough to receive it**.

So, what are you doing during your waiting season? Are you complaining, growing weary, or doubting God's goodness? Or are you leaning into His presence, asking Him to reveal what He wants you to learn, how He wants you to grow?

Matthew 6:33 reminds us, *"Seek first the kingdom of God and His righteousness, and all these things will be added to you."*

Your waiting period isn't wasted; it's an opportunity. Use it to draw closer to God, to develop the skills, the patience, and the character you'll need when your prayer is answered.

The next time you ask God for something, pause and reflect: **Am I truly ready for what I'm asking for?**

God's timing is always perfect. If you're faithful in the waiting and diligent in your preparation, what He has for you will come at the right moment. Trust Him: He knows exactly what you need and when you need it.

Pray with me

Lord,

Lord, help me to use this waiting season to grow in faith and prepare for what You have planned. Teach me to trust Your timing and align my heart with Your will.

In Jesus' name,
Amen.

Day 63

Letting Go and Trusting God's Plan

Not everyone can go where God is taking you. Along this journey, you may lose people, places, and things: not in a tragic way, but in a way that requires you to close the door and let God seal it shut. It doesn't mean those people or experiences weren't important. They were. They played a role in your story, but the life God has planned for you doesn't include them moving forward, and that's okay.

Letting go is never easy. Losing what feels familiar; whether it's relationships, routines, or even places, can feel scary. It's often the uncertainty that holds us back, leaving us clinging to what's known, even when it no longer fits where God is leading us. But here's the truth: The key to your freedom has always been in your possession.

There's a popular saying: *Some people are in your life for a reason, some for a season, and others for a lifetime.* The challenge is discerning who and what belongs in each category, and being willing to release the things God is calling you to let go of.

Sometimes we cling to things that no longer serve us. Maybe it's a table you're no longer invited to sit at. A relationship that's run its course. A job that doesn't align with your calling anymore. God has a way of gently tapping us on the shoulder to say, **"It's time to move on."**

Here's a simple analogy: Imagine me walking around my neighborhood wearing my daughter's small T-shirt, when I typically wear an XL, sometimes even an XXL: what would you think? Can you picture how ridiculous that would look? A shirt that's four sizes too small, squeezing the life out of me. Everyone around me would immediately know it doesn't fit, yet I'd keep wearing it, convincing myself it still works.

That's exactly how some of us are living: clinging to things that no longer fit. **We hold onto outdated relationships, missed opportunities, and situations that hinder our growth.** These "small T-shirts" are weighing us down, keeping us from stepping into the fullness of what God has already prepared. It's time to let go of the things that don't serve you, and boldly embrace the life that God is calling you into. The right fit is waiting: don't settle for less than what He has for you.

When God calls us to step into His plans, it often feels overwhelming. The obstacles ahead can seem too big, too impossible. But look at David. He was just a shepherd boy, overlooked and underestimated. Yet, when Goliath towered over him, mocking him and his people, David didn't flinch.

Why? Because David didn't trust in his own strength, **he trusted in God's.**

David declared, *"You come to me with a sword and with a spear and with a javelin, but I come to you in the name of the Lord of hosts"* (1 Samuel 17:45). Armed with nothing but a sling, five smooth stones, and unwavering faith, David defeated the giant.

David's victory wasn't about **his size or skill**. It was about his trust in God's power.

Now, take a moment. Look in the mirror. Remind yourself who you are: **You are more than a conqueror. You are chosen by God to do great works.** The same God who empowered David to defeat Goliath is with you, ready to help you overcome the giants in your life.

It's easy to want to go back to the familiar because it feels safe. But remember Lot's wife: she looked back and turned into a pillar of salt. Some of us are still looking back, trapped in the very places God is trying to free us from.

So, I ask you: **What is God asking you to let go of?** How many signs or people will God send to get your attention? God is trying to take you beyond your wildest dreams, but He can't do it if you keep holding onto what He's called you to release.

When God called Joshua to step into his destiny, He said: *"Be strong and courageous. Do not be afraid; do not be discouraged, for the Lord your God will be with you wherever you go"* (Joshua 1:9).

What are you holding onto that God has asked you to release? Are you running from His call like Jonah? Is fear holding you back from starting that business, forgiving someone, or leaving a job that no longer aligns with your purpose?

I get it. I've been a runner, too. Afraid to trust God fully, afraid to step out in faith. But I'm here to tell you: **there's freedom on the other side of obedience.**

Today is the day you break free. Today is the day you stop making excuses. Today is the day you let go and let God.

You can trust Him. He will never fail you. The life He has planned for you is beyond anything you can imagine.

Take that first step. Look in the mirror, and say it out loud: "I am more than a conqueror. I am chosen by God to do great works."

Now believe it. Walk in it. Live it.

Pray with me

Lord,

Give me the strength to let go of what no longer fits, the courage to walk where You're leading, and the faith to trust that what's ahead is better than what's behind. I choose to follow You.

In Jesus' name,
Amen.

Whose Voice Are You Listening To?

A few days ago, I was writing a blog I thought would inspire others, but something felt off. As I read it aloud, my daughter, sitting across from me, interrupted with a knowing smile:

"Dad, it's obvious you don't like it."

I looked at her and asked why she thought that. She smiled and said, **"Because you're asking me too many questions about it, and you never do that."**

She was right. I didn't like it because I wasn't writing from my heart. I was trying to force something that wasn't God-breathed.

In 2008, I was offered a high-powered job at a company everyone said was on the verge of bankruptcy. **"Don't take it,"** they warned. **"It's a sinking ship."** Their voices were loud, but God's voice was louder. I kept hearing Him telling me to accept the job.

I wrestled with the decision night and day, torn between logic and faith. Ultimately, I chose to trust God's voice. I took the job.

Three months later, the company shut down. I was unemployed, and the enemy wasted no time filling my mind with doubt: **Maybe they were right. Maybe you heard wrong.**

But I held onto God's promise, even in the storm. I knew He had a plan.

For the next nine months, I worked three jobs, seven days a week, 70-80 hours a week: making only a fraction of my previous salary. It was exhausting, humbling, and at times discouraging. But through it all, I kept trusting God. I clung to His voice, refusing to let the enemy's lies shake my faith.

And then, one day, the phone rang. A major corporation offered me a job I never expected: one that exceeded anything I could have dreamed of. It was more responsibility, more opportunity, and more income than I had ever imagined.

God proved, once again, that His plans are perfect. He took what looked like a setback and turned it into a setup for something greater.

I'm glad I listened to His voice. That decision changed my life.

God's voice will lead you to places you can't see yet, places that defy logic and challenge your understanding. But He is faithful. He will never fail or abandon you.

Maybe you're facing a tough decision right now. Maybe you're wrestling with the voices of fear, doubt, or well-meaning people telling you what to do. Maybe you're caught between what makes sense and what God is calling you to do.

Here's my advice: **Be still and know that He is God. Trust His voice.**

From the beginning, humanity has struggled to trust God's voice. Think of Adam and Eve. The serpent convinced Eve that God's truth wasn't enough, and she reached for what wasn't hers. Adam followed. In that moment of disobedience, everything changed, not because God stopped loving them, but because they chose the wrong voice.

Jesus said, **"My sheep know My voice."** But the enemy works tirelessly to distract and deceive us, using fear, comfort, and worldly pleasures to pull us away from God's plans.

The mind is a battlefield. The stakes are high, and the choice is yours: Will you follow the wide road, filled with distractions, or the narrow road, where God's purpose and promises are waiting?

When I reflect on that season in 2008, I'm reminded that God's plans often don't make sense in the moment. But His ways are higher, His timing perfect, and His love unwavering.

If I had listened to the wrong voices, I would have missed the blessing God had in store for me. If I had let fear win, I would have settled for less than His best.

Maybe you're in a similar place right now. Maybe you're doubting, second-guessing, or struggling to hear God through the noise. Let me remind you:

God knows you. He sees you. He has a plan for you.

He knows your flaws, your doubts, and your fears, and He loves you anyway. His love is steadfast, even when you stumble. He pursues you, even when you wander. He redeems what feels broken and makes all things new.

God is calling you to something greater. The question is: **Whose voice will you listen to?**

You don't have to have all the answers. You don't have to see the full picture. All you have to do is trust Him.

The nations are waiting. There are lives that will be changed because of your obedience. Don't let fear, indecision, or the opinions of others hold you back. Take the first step.

Your destiny is waiting. God is with you. Trust His voice.

Pray with me

Lord,

Quiet the noise around me so I can hear You clearly. When fear and doubt try to lead me, remind me of Your faithfulness. Give me the courage to trust Your voice: even when it doesn't make sense. I believe You have a plan, and I choose to follow You.

In Jesus' name,
Amen.

Day 65

What's Stopping You From Becoming the Best Version of Yourself?

What's holding you back? Fear? Doubt? A voice in your head whispering, You're not enough? Maybe you're standing on the edge of your destiny but too afraid to leap. Are you stuck in a job, relationship, or situation that God's been calling you to leave behind?

Fear has a way of paralyzing us. It convinces us that our dreams are impossible, that we're unworthy of the life God planned for us. But here's the truth: until you believe God's promises for your life, you'll never fully step into the abundance He has for you.

I've been there. I know what it's like to feel stuck, staring at the life I prayed for but unable to take the first step. Fear told me I didn't have what it takes. Faith whispered back, ***"You can do all things through Christ who strengthens you"*** **(Philippians 4:13)**. It wasn't easy, but I chose to trust God, and everything changed.

Think back to your childhood. Remember the question adults loved to ask: "What do you want to be when you grow up?"

Maybe you dreamed of being a doctor, teacher, artist, or someone extraordinary. But along the way, someone may have told you those dreams were impossible, and you believed them. Did you settle for less than what God created you for?

What if I told you that everything you've prayed for is waiting on the other side of fear? What if unlocking your destiny means activating the faith that's already inside you?

The Bible tells us, ***"If you have faith as small as a mustard seed, you can say to this mountain, 'Move from here to there,' and it will move"*** **(Matthew 17:20)**. A mustard seed is only 1–2 millimeters in size, yet God says that's all the faith we need for miracles. Faith isn't about being fearless: it's about trusting God enough to take the first step.

Fear, on the other hand, does more than keep us stuck. It steals our joy, clouds our thinking, and separates us from God. The more we feed fear, the louder it grows. But here's the key: whatever you feed will grow. If you feed your faith, it will flourish. If you trust God in the face of fear, you'll experience the breakthrough you've been waiting for.

Here's where it starts:
1. **Stop seeking approval from the wrong people.** Not everyone in your life deserves access to your dreams. Judas walked with Jesus, yet he betrayed Him. Guard your heart and trust that God will place the right people in your life at the right time.
2. **Shift your focus to God's Word.** When fear tries to overwhelm you, speak God's promises over your life. ***"For God has not given us a spirit of fear, but of power and of love and of a sound mind"*** **(2 Timothy 1:7)**.

3. **Take one small step of faith.** Maybe it's a phone call, a decision, or simply spending time in prayer. Faith grows when you act on it. Remember, even small steps move you closer to your destiny.

4. **Pray for strength and clarity.** Ask God to help you see the situation through His eyes. *"Trust in the Lord with all your heart and lean not on your own understanding"* (**Proverbs 3:5**).

Fear will tell you to settle, but faith reminds you that you are more than a conqueror **(Romans 8:37).** God's plans for your life are bigger than your fears, no matter your age or circumstances. Faith calls you to rise above fear and step boldly into the life He created for you.

What if everything you're going through right now is preparing you for what you prayed for? The challenges, obstacles, and even failures are part of God's refining process. David faced Goliath, armed only with a sling and faith. Jesus fed over 5,000 with just five loaves and two fish. Miracles happen when faith leads.

You are the miracle. God sees greatness in you, even if you don't see it yet. Trust Him. His love for you is perfect, and *"Perfect love casts out fear"* (**1 John 4:18**). Take the first step, no matter how small.

God is waiting for you on the other side of fear. Your best life: the life He planned for you before the foundation of the world is within reach. Feed your faith, move the mountain, and step into the extraordinary.

Pray with me

Lord,

I've let fear hold me back for too long. Today, I choose to trust You more than my doubts. Give me the courage to take the first step, even if it's small. Remind me that Your plans are good, and Your love casts out all fear. I believe You're with me, and I'm ready to move forward.

In Jesus' name,
Amen.

Day 66

The Power of Words:
Building Up or Tearing Down

"Sticks and stones may break my bones, but words will never hurt me."

If you've ever heard that saying, you might have believed it: just like I did when I was a child. But life has a way of showing us the truth. Words hurt. Sometimes, they hurt more than any physical wound ever could. Words can cut deep, leaving scars we carry for years.

I know this because I've lived it.

Growing up, I was picked on a lot because of my dark complexion. People called me cruel names, each one more hurtful than the last. At just ten years old, I couldn't understand why. All I knew was that those words wounded me in ways I couldn't explain. They made me question my worth, my identity, and my place in the world.

One day, a classmate laughed and said, "You'll never be anything but a shadow." That moment stayed with me. It wasn't just the words but the certainty with which they were spoken. It felt like a verdict, as if my future had been decided.

I began to tell myself, **Maybe they're right. Maybe there's something wrong with me.** Those words planted seeds of doubt, and I unknowingly watered them with fear and insecurity. I didn't talk to anyone about it. Instead, I fought back with my fists and silent battles in my mind.

But here's the truth: the real fight wasn't with those kids who hurt me. The real fight was inside me. It was a battle for my heart, my identity, and my future.

Looking back, I see now how powerful words are. The words spoken to me as a child tried to define me. And for a while, they succeeded.

But here's what I've learned: Words don't just come from others. **Some of the most powerful words we hear are the ones we speak to ourselves.** The words we say about who we are, what we're worth, and what we're capable of, they shape us. They have the power to imprison us or set us free.

Proverbs 18:21 says, *"The tongue has the power of life and death, and those who love it will eat its fruit."* Every word we speak is a seed. It's either a seed of life or destruction. **And eventually, we'll eat the fruit of what we plant.** When I read that verse, it struck me: I had been eating the bitter fruit of my own negative words for years.

For a long time, I let negativity win. The words spoken over me by others, and by myself, kept me locked in a cycle of self-doubt.

But then, something changed.

It wasn't immediate, and it wasn't easy. But I realized I had a choice. I couldn't control the words others said about me, but I could control the words I spoke over myself. I could uproot the seeds of doubt and plant something better.

So, I started speaking life over myself. I began to say things like, **You are worthy. You are loved. You are chosen by God.** At first, it felt strange: like I was lying to myself. But over time, those words began to take root.

The more I spoke life, the more I believed it. And as I believed it, my world began to change. God started to use me in ways I never thought possible. What had once been a source of pain became a testimony of His power to heal and transform.

Here's what I want you to know: the same power that transformed my life is available to you. God created each of us with purpose, love, and intention. He gave us the ability to speak life, not just over ourselves but over the people and situations around us.

When we align our words with His truth, amazing things happen. We stop believing the lies the world tells us, and we start living in the fullness of who God made us to be.

But it starts with a **choice**.

You have to choose to speak life. You have to choose to see yourself as God sees you: fearfully and wonderfully made, full of potential, and capable of greatness.

When I look back on my journey, I see how much words shaped my life. The negative words tried to define me, but they didn't have the final say. God did.

And He says the same about you.

You are not the names others have called you. You are not the mistakes you've made. You are not the lies you've believed. You are a child of God, chosen for a purpose, and equipped with the power to change your life: and the lives of those around you, through your words.

So today, I leave you with this question: **What kind of seeds are you planting with your words?**

The choice is yours. Speak life, and watch God transform your world.

Pray with me

Lord,

You know the words that hurt me: the ones I've carried for way too long. I don't want to hold onto them anymore. I give them to You. Help me believe what You say about me. That I'm loved. Chosen. Worth it. Made on purpose. From now on, I want to speak life over myself and others. Let my words reflect Your heart.

In Jesus' name,
Amen.

Day 67

The Life-Changing Power of Forgiveness

Forgiveness is one of the most powerful gifts God gives us. It's not just a way to release others, it's the way to **release yourself from pain, anger, and hurt**. When you forgive those who have hurt you, betrayed your trust, broken your heart, or hurt someone you love: you're choosing freedom for yourself.

Let me be clear: Forgiveness doesn't mean you forget what happened. It doesn't mean you're saying it's okay. It means you choose to **let go of the poison** of anger and bitterness. So many people hold onto unforgiveness, not realizing that it traps them in pain and stops them from moving forward in life.

I know this from experience. I haven't always been the man I am today. I've made mistakes: things I regret. I've hurt people. But I've also been hurt. There were times when I wanted to get back at people who betrayed me or hurt me. I wanted to fight back.

But then I thought about Jesus.

When Jesus was hanging on the cross, He was in unimaginable pain. He had been wrongfully accused and was dying for sins He didn't commit. Yet, in that moment, He prayed, **"Father, forgive them, for they know not what they do."**

Let that sink in. Jesus didn't just forgive those who wronged Him, He prayed for their forgiveness. This isn't the forgiveness of someone who has a peaceful, easy life. This is the forgiveness of a man who is dying for the sins of the world; yet still, in the midst of His agony, He chooses to forgive.

Holding onto unforgiveness is like drinking poison and hoping it hurts the other person. The truth is, it only hurts you. It keeps you stuck, angry, and trapped. It steals your peace and joy. But the moment you choose to forgive, you can begin to heal and feel free.

I know it's hard. I know it feels unfair. But forgiveness isn't about forgetting the hurt. It's about choosing to free yourself from the pain.

I've been there. Before my father passed away, I carried so much bitterness toward him. The words that were left unsaid, the years of pain, the anger I felt… it was killing me. But when I gave my life to Christ, everything shifted. God gave me the courage to face that anger head-on. I had a real conversation with my father, one where I poured out my heart, my hurt, and my forgiveness. And in that moment, when I chose to forgive him: **I was freed. Both of us were freed.**

Who do you need to forgive? Who do you need to ask forgiveness from?

As long as there is breath in your lungs, there is still time. Forgiveness is hard, but it's life-changing. When you forgive, you open the door for healing, peace, and freedom. It doesn't just heal the relationship with the other person; **it heals you**. It allows you to grow, to move forward, and to experience God's peace in your heart.

You see, forgiveness isn't just a choice between you and the person who hurt you. It's also a choice to trust God. To let Him handle the justice, and to surrender your pain into His hands. When we forgive, we trust that God sees our hurt, He understands our pain, and He will bring healing and justice in His time.

Jesus died for our sins: sins we could never repay. He showed us the ultimate example of forgiveness. When we choose to forgive, we're following His example and opening our hearts to healing. We stop carrying the weight of bitterness, and we let God replace it with peace.

Don't wait another day. Don't let the poison of unforgiveness continue to steal your peace, your joy, and your life. The moment you choose to forgive, God will meet you there, and He will begin to heal the brokenness inside of you.

You've got this. And I am so proud of you for making the choice to forgive. Remember, forgiveness is not just a choice; it is a step toward the amazing life that God has for you. **So, let go. Release it. And embrace the freedom that comes when you choose to forgive: just as Christ has forgiven you.**

Pray with me

Lord,

You know the hurt I've been carrying. You know what they did and how it made me feel. I've held onto the pain, but I'm tired of carrying it. I want to be free.

Today, I choose to forgive. Not because it was okay, but because I don't want to live stuck anymore. I'm trusting You with the pain, the justice, and the healing.

Help me let go. Heal the broken places in me. Teach me to forgive like You do: with grace, mercy, and love.

In Jesus' name,
Amen.

Day 68

When Life Changes, Trust God's Perfect Plan

Life doesn't always go the way we planned. Sometimes, our dreams unravel, our plans fall apart, and we're left wondering, **God, why is this happening to me?**

But here's the truth: God doesn't let things fall apart without a purpose. He's not punishing you or forgetting you. He's redirecting you. What feels like rejection or failure to us is often His way of steering us toward something far better: something only He can see.

Think about a time in your life when you prayed for something with all your heart, only to watch it slip away. Maybe it was a dream job, a relationship you thought would last forever, or an opportunity that felt like everything you'd been working for. The disappointment felt unbearable, didn't it?

But now, looking back, can you see how God used that moment? Maybe the door that closed led you to a new opportunity that fits you perfectly. Or perhaps the heartbreak taught you to rely on Him in ways you never had before. **Romans 8:28** reminds us: *"And we know that in all things God works* *for the good of those who love Him, who have been called according to His purpose."*

God isn't just working in the good times: He's working in the mess, in the disappointment, and in the confusion.

We like to think life is a straight line: we plan, we pray, and things happen just as we imagined. But life is more like a GPS. We may enter a destination, but when we take a wrong turn, or when a road is blocked: the GPS doesn't give up. It recalculates, finding another way to get us where we need to go.

That's exactly how God works. When our plans fall apart, His plans fall into place. **Proverbs 19:21** tells us: *"Many are the plans in a person's heart, but it is the Lord's purpose that prevails."*

What feels like a detour to us is often part of His perfect design.

Trusting God in the middle of change isn't easy. It takes faith to believe He's working when we can't see the full picture.

It's natural to feel disappointed when life doesn't go your way. But instead of holding onto frustration, take it to God. Pray, **"Lord, I trust You. I don't understand, but I know You have a plan for me."** Surrendering your plans doesn't mean giving up, it means trusting God's way is better.

Even when life feels chaotic, God is still in control. He's using every twist and turn to shape you, teach you, and prepare you. Ask yourself, **What might God be teaching me in this season?** Often, the hardest moments hold the greatest lessons.

You don't need to have everything figured out. **Psalm 119:105** says, ***"Your word is a lamp for my feet, a light on my path."*** Notice it doesn't say the whole path will be lit: just the next step. Trust God enough to take that step, even when you can't see the final destination.

It's hard to understand why God allows certain things to happen. But one thing is certain: He is good, and His plan is perfect. **Jeremiah 29:11** promises us, ***"For I know the plans I have for you," declares the Lord, "plans to prosper you and not to harm you, plans to give you hope and a future."***

The next time life doesn't go as planned, take a deep breath and trust that God is in control. Instead of asking, **"Why me?"** ask, **"Lord, what's next?"** He's not done with your story. The very thing you're struggling with today could become the biggest blessing of your life.

Even when the road feels uncertain, God is guiding you. His plan is always greater than anything you could imagine. Trust Him.

Pray with me

Lord,

This isn't what I expected. Things didn't go the way I hoped, and honestly, it's hard to understand why. But I know You're still with me, even in the confusion.

Help me trust You when the plan changes. Remind me that You're not punishing me: you're guiding me. Show me what You're doing, even if it's just the next step.

I surrender my plans to You. I believe Your way is better. Even when I can't see the full picture, I know You're working all things for good.

In Jesus' name,
Amen.

Day 69

You Are Worthy of the Call

Have you ever felt like you're on a treadmill, running faster and faster but going nowhere? You've been pouring your heart and soul into your dreams, but it feels like you're hitting a brick wall. Discouragement creeps in, and you start to question if your efforts are even worth it.

But I'm here to tell you: **don't give up.**

In moments of doubt and uncertainty, it's easy to forget one truth that remains constant: **God is with you.** No matter where you are, no matter what you're facing, He is by your side, guiding, supporting, and lifting you up. You are never alone. **His presence is with you every step of the way,** even in the most challenging of times.

There are days when life feels overwhelming, and we wonder if we're on the right path. It's easy to think we're not worthy of God's calling, or that we've strayed too far to be used for His purpose. But I want to remind you today: **You are worthy.** You were created with a purpose, a divine calling that no one can take away. **God's love for you is unconditional**: it is not based on your past mistakes or failures. His plan for your life is good, and He has equipped you for it, every step of the way.

No matter how hard the journey gets, remember that **God has never, and will never, leave you.** His promise to be with you is unbreakable, and it's in His strength that you will find the courage to keep moving forward. There is nothing in this world that can separate you from His love. **Your life is a beautiful testimony of His grace, and He has uniquely equipped you to fulfill the call on your life.**

Don't let doubt or fear hold you back. **Step into your purpose with confidence**, knowing that you are **worthy of the call God has placed on your life.** Embrace His love, trust in His timing, and walk boldly into the life He's destined you to lead.

You are worthy. You are loved. You are never alone. God is with you, always.

Don't let discouragement write the end of your story.

You were created on purpose, for a purpose, and God has not changed His mind about you. Even when it feels like nothing is moving, heaven is still working. Keep going. Keep trusting. Keep believing that God is with you and that His plan is still unfolding.

"So do not throw away your confidence; it will be richly rewarded." **(Hebrews 10:35)**

"Being confident of this, that he who began a good work in you will carry it on to completion until the day of Christ Jesus." **(Philippians 1:6)**

You are not running in vain. You are not forgotten.

Pray with me

Lord,

Sometimes I feel like I'm giving my all and getting nowhere. It's hard. I get tired. I start to wonder if I'm even on the right path. But today, I choose to believe You're with me.

Remind me that I'm not alone. That I'm not forgotten. That You're still working, even when I can't see it.

Help me walk in the purpose You've placed on my life. Give me the strength to keep going, the faith to trust Your timing, and the courage to believe I am worthy, because You say I am.

In Jesus' name,
Amen.

Day 70

Awaken Your True Calling:
The Mission Inside You

What if the one thing you're meant to do in life has the power to change not only your world, but the world around you?

What if your life wasn't just a series of random events? What if it was a mission: a force waiting to change everything? **What would your mission statement be?**

The great *Martin Luther King Jr.* once said, **"If a man has not discovered what he will die for, he is not fit to live."** That statement isn't just profound; it's a wake-up call. What is your purpose? What's worth fighting for? What would you put it all on the line for?

Martin Luther King Jr. knew his mission, and Jesus did too. But what about you?

I'm not asking you to compare yourself to them. They had their path, and you have yours. But make no mistake, **you have a mission too**. You've always had it. It's not about becoming someone else. **It's about becoming the fullest version of you**.

Look deep inside yourself. What is the one thing that excites you, that calls to you, that makes you feel alive? If you're a parent, maybe it's giving your children a life better than the one you had. Maybe it's helping your community or supporting those you love. Or maybe it's something that lives only in your heart: **a dream, a vision, a desire**.

Think back to when you were younger. What did you want to be before fear had a chance to speak? What did you dream about before doubt settled in? **What would you do if you weren't afraid?**

Maybe your mission is to live boldly, to unlock your full potential, and to inspire others to do the same. What are you loyal to? What would you stand for, even when the world says it's impossible?

Ask yourself: **What would you do for free?** The answer is already inside you. The truth of who you're meant to be has been planted in your soul from the moment you were born. Over the years, you've watered it: sometimes without even knowing it. Maybe life got in the way or fear caused you to set it aside, but it's always there, waiting for you to reclaim it. A memory, a thought, a small spark; sometimes that's all it takes to reconnect you to that dream.

But here's the real question: **Why did you stop pursuing it?**

For me, growing up, we didn't have much. But I had something far more powerful: a deep conviction that there was something within me that needed to awaken. I watched my mother raise five kids on her own, working three jobs to provide.

Her strength ignited something in me; it told me that I had a purpose, that I wasn't just surviving, but I was meant to thrive.

And let me tell you: It's not just in a few of us, **it's in all of us**. That fire, that purpose? **It's inside you too.**

No matter the struggles you've faced: financial hardship, loss, rejection, or fear, those are not the things that define you. They are the building blocks of your story. Every obstacle, every setback, is pushing you closer to your true mission. Those challenges aren't the end of your story; they're shaping you into the person you were meant to become.

For me, I always dreamed of being an author. And I achieved that. But I didn't stop there. I see myself as a *New York Times* bestselling author. It hasn't happened yet, but I know it will. I've seen it in my dreams. And you have your own vision, don't you? A dream, a passion, a mission that's been quietly waiting for you to return to it.

Your story isn't over. It's just in a different chapter. **Every day is an opportunity to move closer to your true purpose.** And the best part? You're still writing your story.

So, don't you dare give up. Don't bury that dream. Fight for it. If you need clarity, pray for it. Ask God to reveal what's been hidden, to guide your steps, because everything you need is already inside of you. You've had it all along.

I live each day with one mission: to become the person I was created to be, to unlock my potential, and to inspire others to do the same. And you have that same power. You will become the person you were meant to be. You already have everything you need to succeed.

Why do I know this? Because God says so. In **Jeremiah 29:11**, He promises: *"For I know the plans I have for you," declares the Lord, "plans to prosper you and not to harm you, plans to give you a hope and a future."* Those aren't just words: **they are the truth.**

Trust God. Trust the plans He has for your life. And become who He created you to be.

Pray with me

Lord,

There's something in me that refuses to settle: something You placed in me from the beginning. I may not see the whole picture, but I know You created me with purpose. I know I'm here for more than just survival. I'm here to make a difference. Awaken what's been buried. Breathe life back into the dreams I've put aside. Show me who I really am and what I'm called to do. Remove the fear, the doubt, the hesitation, and replace it with boldness, clarity, and conviction.

I don't want to live safe. I want to live surrendered. Help me chase the mission You've given me with passion, discipline, and faith. I say yes to the call. I say yes to becoming who You created me to be.

In Jesus' name,
Amen.

Day 71

Believe Beyond the Surface

Everything isn't always as it appears. Sometimes, we need to look beyond the surface and trust in what's unseen.

In 2017, I was outside raking leaves from my yard, which honestly looked more like a weed pit than anything else. Just as I was making some progress, my neighbor walked over. I'd recently moved in, so I assumed he was coming to introduce himself. After a brief hello, he looked around, chuckled, and said, **"The neighbors call this yard a weed pit. It's going to take a miracle to fix it up."**

I turned to him and smiled. **"I believe in miracles,"** I replied.

In that moment, I had two choices: I could believe him, or I could believe in something bigger.

I chose faith.

Soon after, a friend came over with his machinery and helped dig up all the weeds in both the front and back yards. We spread grass seed and covered it with hay. But it wasn't easy going: birds kept landing in the yard and feasting on the seeds. Every day, I'd chase them off, laughing at myself as I imagined my neighbors watching, probably recording me for social media. It was a sight, I'm sure.

Around that time, I also had an irrigation system installed, hoping it would speed up the process. But after a few months, there was still no sign of green grass. From time to time, my neighbor would swing by, probably to see if his prediction had come true. Still, I kept believing, even though the results weren't immediate.

Nine months passed, and the yard still looked pretty bare. But I kept working, kept watering, kept shooing away those birds. I even wore a shirt that read, **"Jesus is enough."** Every time I looked down at it, it was like a reminder to keep going.

Finally, in the summer of 2018, I saw the first, delicate blades of grass starting to peek through the soil. It wasn't until the following spring that my yard flourished. By then, I had the greenest grass in the entire neighborhood.

One day, that same neighbor stopped by. This time, he looked around in awe and said, **"Wow, your yard looks amazing."**

I just smiled and replied, **"I told you I believe in miracles."**

Sometimes, life can look just like my yard did: barren, unpromising, maybe even a bit hopeless. But when you trust in God and believe that He is at work, nothing and no one can hold you back. **Matthew 19:26** says, *"With man, this is impossible, but with God, all things are possible."*

Whatever you're facing: a dream you've had for years, a new job, your health, or a closer walk with God, remember the story of the weed pit, the doubting voices, the obstacles. They're temporary. Faith without action is empty, but when faith is paired with effort, that's when growth happens. If I had simply believed but hadn't put in the work, my yard would still be a weed pit.

Think about your own **"yard."** What is it that you want to grow? What would it look like if you pushed through the doubts, kept believing, and did the work? You're called to do great things. Believe, put in the work, and watch your life grow.

Faith doesn't always yield immediate results, but strong faith endures testing. So, what is your faith telling you today? **Believe boldly, act with purpose, and watch as faith turns obstacles into miracles.**

Pray with me

Lord,

Thank You for reminding me that even when things look barren, You're still working beneath the surface. Sometimes I can't see the progress, but I choose to believe that growth is happening in ways I don't yet understand.

Help me stay faithful when the wait feels long, when the voices around me speak doubt, and when results don't come right away. Give me the strength to keep showing up, to keep planting, watering, and trusting.

I believe in miracles, and I believe in You. No matter what it looks like today, I trust that You're making something beautiful grow in my life.

In Jesus' name,
Amen.

Day 72

Burning the Candle at Both Ends

Have you ever felt like you're constantly in motion, but not really getting anywhere? The saying **"burning the candle at both ends"** captures this perfectly: it's about sacrificing rest and well-being in pursuit of productivity, achievement, or even just staying above water.

When was the last time you truly rested, with a full 8 hours of sleep? When was the last time you disconnect from the chaos around you? When was the last time you took time just for yourself? Sometimes, the worries and stresses of life make us feel like hamsters on a wheel: running as fast as we can, but never actually moving forward. Or, imagine your life as an hourglass. The sand is full at the top, but the moment you flip it, time begins slipping away, grain by grain. We rush through the day, often without a clear destination in mind.

Let me share a story. One day, a friend called to tell me about a dream they had involving me. In the dream, I was on a racetrack with other runners. The race began, and I found myself jumping from lane to lane. **"Run!"** my friend shouted from the sidelines, but I kept repeating, **"I don't know what lane I**

belong in!" The race continued, and I was still there, confused and unsure. My friend yelled, **"Just run!"**

The lesson here is simple but profound: I wasn't lost because I couldn't run; I was lost because I didn't know where I was supposed to be. In life, are you running in the right lane? Do you even know which lane is yours? Or are you, like that hamster, burning out on endless cycles with no true destination?

There are only 24 hours in each day. How you choose to spend them determines the race you're running. Pouring into others is a beautiful act, but pouring into yourself is not just an option, it's a necessity.

1 Corinthians 6:19-20 reminds us that our bodies are temples of the Holy Spirit. We are not our own; we were bought at a price. When you neglect your well-being, you are not only doing a disservice to yourself but to the Creator who entrusted you with the gift of life. Taking care of yourself; mind, body, and spirit isn't selfish; it's a way of honoring the life you've been given. Your potential is like a light switch in a dark room. You have the power to illuminate your path, but you have to recognize that the power is within you.

Today, do something that feeds your soul, unapologetically. Take a moment to rest, recharge, and remember that your well-being is the foundation of all you hope to achieve. You deserve it. Imagine stepping off that wheel and finding clarity in the stillness. The time you give yourself will never be wasted: it will be the key to unlocking a life full of purpose and joy, as God intended.

Don't wait for the perfect moment, because that moment might never come. Make today the day you prioritize yourself. Right now, set aside just five minutes: pause, breathe, and think about what you need. **Commit to doing one thing today that's just for you.**

Flip that hourglass, choose your lane, and run your race; not anyone else's. **Because when you prioritize yourself, the world around you benefits from the best version of you.** Go ahead: flick that light switch. The greatness within you is waiting to shine. **Activate it. Own it. Claim it.**

Remember: Your life, your body, and your time are sacred gifts. Honor them well.

Pray with me

Lord,

I've been running hard, but lately, I don't even know where I'm headed. I'm tired, stretched thin, and craving peace. Help me slow down long enough to hear Your voice and remember what truly matters.

Show me the lane You've called me to. Help me honor my body, my mind, and my time as the sacred gifts they are. Teach me to rest, to reset, and to run my race: not someone else's.

Thank You for reminding me that rest is not weakness, it's worship.

In Jesus' name,
Amen.

Day 73

The Strength to Forgive: Releasing the Past to Embrace a Better Future

People will hurt you: it's a painful, undeniable reality. Sometimes, the people you trust most: family, friends, loved ones, will be the ones who betray you. They might lie about you, attack your character, or spread rumors to anyone who will listen, all to make themselves feel better.

For years, I carried a heavy burden: resentment and bitterness toward my father. He was absent during my childhood, and that absence left scars that I carried into adulthood. I wanted to forgive, but I didn't know how. I held onto the pain because it felt justified, and I was convinced that holding onto that anger protected me from being hurt again. It wasn't until I found Jesus that I realized holding onto the bitterness was hurting me more than it was protecting me. Forgiveness didn't come overnight; it was a process, a journey, but with God's help, I was able to release the pain. My relationship with my father began to heal, and it grew until the day he passed away. Forgiving him didn't change the past, but it changed me. It gave me the freedom to love, to grow, and to move forward without the weight of **what could have been**.

Maybe you're carrying your own heavy burden; whether it's a betrayal that happened last week or a wound that's been with you for years. It may be hard to let go of pain that feels so real and raw. It's tempting to hold onto resentment because it feels like the only way to make sense of what happened. But here's the truth I learned: forgiveness isn't about letting them off the hook: it's about setting yourself free.

In moments of deep hurt, I think about Jesus' words on the Cross in **Luke 23:34**: *"Father, forgive them, for they do not know what they are doing."* If you're struggling with forgiveness, whether it's from a recent betrayal or a long-standing wound, I get it. It feels impossible to let go, especially when you've been hurt over and over again. But forgiveness doesn't excuse what happened; it's a decision to no longer be chained by the pain. It's a declaration that you won't let what happened to you dictate who you are becoming.

Forgiving isn't a one-time act. It's a daily choice: a choice to release the grip of resentment and to refuse to be defined by your past or present hurts. Forgiveness doesn't erase the hurt; it transforms it. It allows you to reclaim your joy and see yourself as more than the sum of your scars. It's about choosing peace over pain, hope over hurt, and healing over bitterness.

Yes, you might lose some relationships along the way. Some people will never understand your choice to forgive, and others will keep believing the lies and rumors spread about you. That's okay. The people who truly belong in your life will see your strength, not your scars. *Maya Angelou* said, **"When people show you who they are, believe them."** Let go of those who've shown themselves unworthy of your trust, and make space for those who will stand by you.

So here's my challenge to you: let go. Let go of the anger, the hurt, the disappointment. Choose to forgive, not because they deserve it, but because you deserve peace. Forgiveness is a decision to break the cycle of pain and to walk in the freedom that God has for you. It's a choice to be stronger than the wounds inflicted upon you. It's about becoming the person you were meant to be, despite what has been done to you.

I believe in you. Even if it's just one small step today, take it. Keep moving forward, and trust that God is with you every step of the way. You are not alone. You are loved, you are valued, and you have a future full of hope and possibility.

Let forgiveness lead you into the life you were always meant to live.

Pray with me

Lord,

You see the pain I've carried: the betrayal, the silence, the words that cut deep. I've tried to protect myself by holding onto anger, but it's only made the wound deeper. Today, I choose to release it. I don't want to carry this anymore.

Help me forgive, not because they were right, but because I want to be free. Heal what still hurts. Fill the spaces left by disappointment with Your peace. Teach me to forgive like You do, one step at a time. I trust You with my healing.

**In Jesus' name,
Amen.**

Perception vs. Reality:
A Lesson in Assumptions

Have you ever assumed something to be true, only to find out later you were wrong? Maybe someone told you something negative about another person, and you believed it without knowing all the facts. We've all been there. Sometimes, people throw stones at you based on how others feel about you, not who you truly are.

I remember one day at the gym. While working out, I noticed this guy staring at me. At first, I let it go, but his stares grew more intense, so I decided to confront him. "**Why are you staring at me?**" I asked.

His response shocked me. "**What makes you think I'm staring at you?**" he said. "**I happen to be looking in your direction, but I wasn't focused on you. I just have a lot on my mind.**"

Immediately, I apologized. He was right. I had made an assumption without knowing the truth. Sound familiar?

That day, I was reminded of an important lesson: **perception is not always reality.**

Assumptions are dangerous, especially when they lead to harmful words. How many times have we judged someone: a family member, friend, or coworker, without knowing their full story? We may hear a negative report and accept it as fact, spreading that opinion through gossip or careless words. But those assumptions can tear people down.

Think about a time when someone spread something untrue about you. It hurt, didn't it? Words, once spoken, cannot be taken back, and they can do real damage. **Proverbs 18:21** reminds us that **the tongue has the power of life and death**. We can either speak life or destruction over people.

Before you make an assumption or pass along a negative report, pause and ask yourself: **Do I know the full story? Am I honoring God with my words?**

Gossip can feel harmless, but it's deadly. Sometimes we don't even realize we're doing it. It starts with a casual observation or sharing what we've heard, but these small moments can snowball into bigger issues, creating misunderstandings and hurt.

Negative talk not only hurts the person being spoken about: it harms us as well. It can poison our hearts, damage our relationships, and distances us from God. When we speak ill of others or spread unverified rumors, we aren't walking in love or truth.

This message isn't just about how others treat us, it's also about how we treat others. How often do we speak without fully understanding someone's situation? Whether it's a family member who seems distant or a coworker who acts difficult, we can be quick to label without knowing their struggles.

We have the choice every day to view people through the lens of grace. The way we speak about our friends, family members, and coworkers reflects what's truly in our hearts.

There will be times when we say or think things about others that may or may not be true. But in those moments, we need to ask ourselves: Is God pleased with how I'm speaking about this person?

Next time you're tempted to make an assumption or believe someone's negative opinion, pause. Take a step back and ask God to show you the truth, not just about the other person, but also about yourself.

All of God's children are all wonderfully made in His image, **including those we're tempted to speak negatively about**. The next time you hear a negative report or are tempted to label someone, be the one who rises above. Choose to reflect the heart of God by speaking truth, kindness, and hope. You have the power to uplift, inspire, and heal with your words.

Step boldly into that truth, and let your words be a beacon of light in a world that desperately needs it. You were made for this.

Pray with me

Lord,

Help me pause before I assume. Teach me to see people the way You see them, not through rumors, hurts, or half-truths, but through grace. Guard my mouth from careless words, and purify my heart from judgment.

Let my words bring healing, not harm. And when I get it wrong, give me the humility to make it right. Use my voice to build others up, not tear them down.

In Jesus' name,
Amen.

Day 75

Faith Through the Silence: How God Transforms Pain into Purpose

Have you ever felt like your entire world collapsed in a single moment? In November 2008, that's exactly what happened to me: losing my job and my dad just five days apart. I had just bought a brand new car, moved into a new house a year earlier, and my daughter's second birthday was just months away. Life, as I knew it, was turned upside down.

My immediate reaction was to be still. I couldn't panic: if I did, everyone around me would too. I'm sure this sounds familiar to many of us. When the weight of the world is on your shoulders, it's natural to feel overwhelmed, ready to throw in the towel. Believe me, I was there. But I knew that panicking wouldn't help. Instead, I decided to act.

Before I talked to anyone, I took my worries to God. I told Him what I was feeling, why I was feeling it, and asked what lesson He wanted me to learn. Honestly, I wanted to blame God, but deep down, I knew I had to seek His guidance instead of pointing fingers.

One of the most difficult parts of that season was how quickly the people around me scattered. When everything was going well, when life was smooth and I was **"up,"** it felt like everyone was close by. But the moment my life took a downturn, people slowly began to drift away. It was painful, but it was in those moments, when I felt alone, that I realized God was calling me to lean on Him more. He wanted my attention, and He got it. **When others disappeared, He remained steadfast.**

Proverbs 3:5-6 reminded me: *"Trust in the LORD with all your heart and lean not on your own understanding; in all your ways submit to him, and he will make your paths straight."*

I had to trust God's plan, even when I couldn't see it clearly.

For the next nine months, I worked three jobs. These were not glamorous positions: most people would have turned their noses up at them, **but I had a family to support**. Pride took a backseat. I worked over 70 hours a week, exhausted, but determined. I had to trust God, even when I couldn't see the light at end of the tunnel.

During those nine months, I was exhausted. There were days when I could barely keep my eyes open. But I kept pushing, knowing that God had a plan for me. I made sure not to complain outwardly, though God and I had many private conversations. And trust me, I didn't win those arguments.

But after those nine long months, **God opened a door.**

Those nine months weren't just a test of endurance, they were a transformation. Every hour I worked, every tear I cried, was shaping me into someone stronger, more resilient, and more trusting of God's plan. **When we surrender to the process, the struggle turns into strength,** and we become the person we were always meant to be.

I passed the test. God had been preparing me all along. When He finally opened that door, His promise was waiting on the other side.

We all face moments where life knocks us down, moments where giving up feels easier than pushing forward. But it's in those moments: when the future is unclear and the path seems darkest, that greatness is born. Sometimes life throws us curveballs we never saw coming, but that doesn't mean **the story is over, it's just beginning.**

So, what's standing between you and your greatness? Is it fear, doubt, or the belief that you're not enough? Let me tell you, there's greatness inside you right now. But you have to believe it, even when the path is uncertain, even when you can't see the next step. Will you choose to rise? Or will you let this moment define you? The choice is yours.

Greatness doesn't come from smooth paths or easy decisions: **it comes from surrendering to the higher calling on your life.** It's realizing that your challenges are not here to break you, but to build you into someone who can carry out a purpose far beyond yourself.

Whatever you're going through right now, no matter how difficult or hopeless things may seem, remember that God is carrying you. Like in the poem Footprints in the Sand, when you can't walk anymore, He's carrying you through the storm.

You are not defined by what happens to you. You are defined by how you rise in response. So when life knocks you down, remember this: God is not finished with you yet. The greatness that lies within you is waiting to be awakened, but only you can make that choice. You are stronger than you know, and your best life is still ahead.

Trust the process, embrace the struggle, and walk boldly into the greatness that's waiting for you.

Pray with me

Lord,

When life feels like it's falling apart, remind me that You are still holding it all together. In the loss, in the waiting, in the moments I don't understand, help me trust You anyway. Give me the strength to keep moving, the faith to keep believing, and the peace to know that You're working even when I can't see it.

Refine me in the struggle. Grow me through the pain. And when the time is right, open the doors You've already prepared for me. I trust You with my process, my purpose, and my future.

In Jesus' name,
Amen.

Protect Your Mind: Your Thoughts Shape Every Part of Your Life

How many times have you said, **"Thank God it's Friday"**? For many of us, it's the anthem of survival. The weekend represents an escape: time to rest, check off errands, or connect with loved ones. But then Sunday night rolls around, and we begin the mental battle of facing another week.

I used to do the same thing, until I had a dream that changed my perspective. In this dream, I was sitting in my doctor's office, and he looked me in the eye and said, over and over, **"Protect your mind, Ron. Protect your mind at all costs."** When I woke up, I couldn't shake the message. What did it mean to truly protect my mind?

Then the answer came. **Proverbs 4:23** declares: *"Be careful what you think, because your thoughts run your life."*

Pause and really consider that: **Your thoughts run your life**. Every day, we are flooded with thoughts; positive, negative, indifferent. But are you aware of the power they hold over every area of your life? Are your thoughts steering you toward the life you desire, or are they sabotaging the greatness that God has placed within you?

Take your family, for example. If you constantly think, **"I'm not good enough as a parent, a spouse, or a sibling,"** how do you think those thoughts will affect the way you interact with your loved ones? Negativity spills over. But imagine waking up and affirming, **"I am blessed to be a part of this family, and today, I will pour love into every relationship."** Do you see the difference? That mental shift has the power to transform how you show up for the people who matter most.

The same goes for your job. If you wake up dreading the workday, telling yourself, **"This job is draining, and I'm stuck,"** then that's the energy you're bringing into your work. You can't grow in a career with that mindset. Instead, speak life into your job, even if it's not where you want to be yet. Say, **"Today, I will give my best and position myself for the next level."** Your thoughts are seeds, and they will grow into your future.

What about your health? If you constantly tell yourself, **"I don't have time to work out,"** or **"I can't eat healthy: it's too hard,"** then those thoughts will run your life, keeping you from the energy, vitality, and strength you deserve. Flip the script: **"I am committed to my health because my body is a gift from God. I will honor it with movement and nourishment."** That's how you reclaim control of your fitness and wellness.

Relationships, whether romantic or friendships, thrive on the thoughts we feed into them. If your inner dialogue is filled with doubt: **"They don't really care about me,"** or **"I always mess things up,"** you'll end up sabotaging even the best connections. Protect your mind. Speak into your relationships with love, trust, and confidence: **"I am worthy of love, and I bring value to every relationship I'm in."**

And let's not forget your spiritual life. Building a stronger relationship with God starts with your mind. If you're constantly thinking, **"I'm too busy to pray, I don't have time for God,"** then that distance will grow. But when you shift your thoughts to say, **"My relationship with God is my foundation, and I will invest in it daily,"** you create space for spiritual growth and clarity. God has already equipped you with everything you need; **you just have to tune your mind to hear His voice**.

Your thoughts are at the core of everything. If you constantly surround yourself with negativity; whether from people, social media, or your own self-talk: that's what will dominate your life. But when you protect your mind, feeding it with thoughts of growth, faith, and possibility, you unlock a path to greatness.

Remember this: **You are the protector of your thoughts.** What others say or think about you is powerless until you choose to internalize it. **Don't let anyone else's opinions define who you are or what you're capable of.** You have the authority to decide how you show up in your family, your career, your relationships, your health, and your walk with God.

Not every day will be perfect, and challenges will come. But just because it's cloudy outside doesn't mean you can't shine from within. **You hold the key to your destiny**: it's already in you.

Protect your mind, guard your heart, and walk in the fullness of what God has planned for you. You are capable of greatness in every area of your life. So, starting today, invest in yourself. Choose thoughts that uplift you, that build you, and that propel you toward the life you were created to live.

Romans 12:2: *"Be transformed by the renewing of your mind."*

Pray with me

Lord,

Help me guard my mind against anything that doesn't come from You. Renew my thoughts and align them with Your truth. When doubt speaks, let faith answer. When fear creeps in, remind me of who I am in You. Teach me to recognize harmful patterns and replace them with words of life, peace, and purpose.

I choose to protect my mind, because I know that's where transformation begins.

In Jesus' name,
Amen.

Day 77

Step Into Your Greatness: No More Waiting

It's October 17, 2024, and here I am, sitting with a cup of Peet's coffee, asking myself: Where did the year go? In just a few months, we'll step into 2025. Time is flying, and that's a wake-up call.

I think back to when I was 10 years old. I told myself I'd become a history professor, teaching at the collegiate level. I knew I had a gift for teaching, and I was sure it would be my way of giving back. But just as quickly, I imagined playing for the Boston Celtics, dreaming of a future in the NBA. That dream? It disappeared. But why?

Looking back now, I realize that maybe God had different plans for me. **Proverbs 16:1** says: *"We can make our own plans, but the Lord gives the right answer."* Here's my question for you: Are you truly trusting God with your life? Or are you just drifting through, waiting for something to change?

It's time to wake up. **This is your moment of reckoning.**

What did you dream of becoming when you were younger? A doctor? Lawyer? Teacher? Business owner? Coach? Are you living out that dream today, or have you settled into a life of compromise, telling yourself that "it's too late" or **"too hard"**? Are you working a job that gives you no satisfaction, where you simply go through the motions?

If that's you, it's time to stop lying to yourself. Time is moving, and if you don't take control of your life now, you never will. Another year will come and go, and you'll find yourself still stuck, watching your dreams fade.

Ask yourself: Why didn't I pursue what I was passionate about? Maybe you listened to the wrong voices: voices that told you to "be realistic," or that you weren't good enough. Maybe fear held you back. But here's the truth: You are responsible for your life, and what you do with it from this moment forward. No one else can live your dream for you.

The dreams you had; whether to be a doctor, a lawyer, a teacher, a business owner, or a coach: they're still alive. They haven't died; they've just been waiting for you. They've been delayed, but they are not denied.

So stop sitting on the sidelines of your own life. Get up. Take control. If you want to reignite your passion, it starts with one decision: to take action. Don't wait for the **"right moment."** Don't wait for permission. Don't wait for someone else to see your potential. The only permission you need is your own.

Whatever you want to be, whatever life you've dreamed of, it's still within your reach. But it's not going to happen by accident. You have to decide today. Because tomorrow, and the next day, aren't guaranteed. They belong to God, not to us. What you do have is today: right now, this moment, and what you choose to do with it is what will define your life.

Life doesn't stop until you do. And as long as you're breathing, greatness is still within your grasp. The only thing standing between you and the life you've always wanted is you. You're the one who decides whether you will move forward or stay stuck.

So today, choose to step into the life you were destined for. Choose to live with purpose.

Pray with me

Lord,

Thank You for the dreams You've placed in me. Help me to stop waiting and start moving. Give me courage to pursue the life You've called me to live. I trust that You're not finished with me yet.

In Jesus' name,
Amen.

Day 78

Never Lose Sight of Yourself While Pouring Into Others

Last week, I did something I rarely do: I took two full days off from work, not for anyone else, but for me. I disconnected, recharged, and made space to simply exist without the demands of others. I hit the "reset" button. And here's what I learned: sometimes, we must slow down and reclaim our time. It's not just a luxury, it's essential. In a world that constantly demands more, it's okay, necessary even, to step back and choose you.

If you're someone who endlessly gives: to the point where everyone else thrives except you, listen closely. You're the person people come to when they need advice, support, money, or time. You're their rock. But when was the last time someone asked how you're doing? You can't be everyone's lifeline and leave yourself drowning. You've become the go-to ATM, where others withdraw without ever making a deposit.

I know why you do it: because your heart is big. You care deeply. You give without hesitation because it's who you are. But here's the truth: you are more than what you give. There comes a day when your cup will be empty, and what then? No one can pour from an empty cup, just as no car can run on fumes. You deserve the same level of care, attention, and love that you so freely give to others.

We live in a world that weighs us down with expectation after expectation, but you don't have to carry that weight alone. God invites us to cast our cares on Him. As **1 Peter 5:7** says: ***"Cast all your anxieties on Him, because He cares for you."*** It's a reminder that your burdens aren't meant to be carried alone: lean into that.

Now, let me challenge you. The next time you feel drained, when you know you need a break, take it. Not just physically, but emotionally, spiritually, take a break from the constant demands, the endless obligations. **Prioritize yourself unapologetically.** You are not an option. You are the priority. Do not make the mistake of sidelining your own well-being while lifting up everyone else.

You matter. You are important. Your greatness is not found in how much you can give until you're empty, but in how you balance giving with receiving. Don't ever feel guilty for saying "no." You can't be the foundation for everyone else when no one is building you up.

Step back. Look at your life. See everything in front of you clearly. What no longer serves you, release it. Protect your peace, because it's priceless. You are priceless. And when you start to treat yourself that way, you will step into the greatness that has been waiting for you all along.

Take care of YOU. Let God refill your cup, and watch how the world around you transforms. The greatness within you deserves to be nurtured. Give yourself the best, because you are worthy of nothing less.

This week, don't just keep going: choose to reset. **Block off time in your calendar for you and honor it like an unbreakable appointment.** Let rest be your resistance. Let peace be your priority. And let God refill what life has drained. You don't need permission to pause: you just need the courage to protect your own well-being. **Start now. You're worth it.**

Pray with me

Lord,

Thank You for reminding me that rest is not weakness, it's necessary. I've poured out so much, but today, I pause to be filled by You. Refresh my soul, refill my strength, and help me release what I was never meant to carry.

Teach me to care for myself the way You care for me, with love, grace, and intention. Give me peace in the pause and courage to protect my time, my energy, and my heart. I trust You to restore what I've lost and lead me into balance and wholeness.

In Jesus' name,
Amen.

Stop Settling: Embrace the Greatness God Has Called You To

Fear causes us to settle, accepting lives we don't want, clinging to what's familiar, even when it doesn't serve us. We shrink back because we doubt our worth or don't trust God's promises. This mindset is a trap, one that can rob you of your potential, stunting your growth and keeping you from the extraordinary life that's waiting for you.

Too many are waiting for someone to give them permission to be great. But here's the truth: You don't need permission from anyone, because greatness already lives inside you. God planted it there. **Jeremiah 29:11** declares, *"For I know the plans I have for you," says the Lord, "plans to prosper you and not to harm you, plans to give you hope and a future."*

So, who are you going to believe? The God who created you with purpose, or the voices of those you've let speak doubt and fear into your life? Understand this: the devil doesn't want you to rise. **His mission is to keep you in bondage by whispering lies that you aren't good enough, that you're destined for mediocrity.**

But God's truth is louder than any lie. As an author of several books, I've lived through moments where **I couldn't see beyond my own limitations.** There were times I sabotaged my own potential, afraid to step into the greatness I knew was within me. I remember a day in college, standing with friends, declaring that I would one day write books. And someone laughed. He said it would never happen. In that moment, **I had a choice: to accept the limitation someone else tried to place on me, or to believe in what I knew God had placed in my heart.**

And here's what I've learned: there will always be people: sometimes those closest to you, who will doubt your dreams, who will tell you "you can't." Friends, family, even people in the church. But the only voice that truly matters is God's. He has gifted each one of us with something special: a talent, a purpose, something designed to bring Him glory.

So, what's your gift? What has God called you to that you've been too afraid to pursue? Has fear paralyzed you? Have you convinced yourself that greatness is for other people, but not for you?

Why haven't you given yourself permission to be great?

It's time to stop letting fear hold you hostage. Today is the day to step out in faith and walk in the purpose God has created you for. **No more excuses**. No more holding back. God didn't create you for mediocrity. **He created you for greatness**. It's time to rise. It's time to use the gifts He gave you.

You don't need another confirmation: God already confirmed it when He created you with purpose. Playing small doesn't honor the One who made you. So shift your posture. Walk like someone who knows they're chosen. Get back in the game. Build what God told you to build. Say what He told you to say. It's not arrogance, it's obedience. Heaven is backing you, and fear can't follow where faith is leading. Move.

"Let us throw off everything that hinders… and run with perseverance the race marked out for us" **(Hebrews 12:1).**

"Whatever you do, do it all for the glory of God" **(1 Corinthians 10:31).**

Pray with me

Lord,

I've spent too much time doubting what You've already spoken. Forgive me for shrinking back when You've called me to rise. Today, I surrender fear, comparison, and hesitation at Your feet. Fill me with courage to walk boldly in the purpose You've placed within me. Remind me that I'm not alone, and that Your plans for my life are still alive. Let every step I take bring You glory. May I never again ask for permission to do what You've already graced me to do.

In Jesus' name,
Amen.

Day 80

The Freedom of Not Pleasing Everyone

From the tender age of 10, I was told to stay true to myself and that trying to please everyone is a waste of time. At that young age, I didn't grasp the depth of those words. It wasn't until I faced one of the darkest periods of my life that I understood how crucial this lesson was.

I've always been the kind of person who would give you the shirt off my back, the last dollar in my wallet, and be there whenever you needed me. But when the tables turned, the very people I counted on vanished. I never realized how truly alone I was until I stood in the midst of that solitude. Have you ever found yourself asking, **"What is this life all about? Are there any real people who genuinely care for me?"**

It's often those we trust the most that are the ones who betray us the deepest. They'll smile to your face, but when the chips are down, their true colors emerge. In **Galatians 1:10**, the Apostle Paul said, *"Am I now trying to win the approval of human beings, or of God? Or am I trying to please people? If I were still trying to please people, I would not be a servant of Christ."* It was in my darkest hour that I realized it wasn't the people who had failed me, **it was my misplaced trust in them that brought me here.** Our struggle isn't against flesh and blood but against the unseen forces that influence our world.

Like Peter from the Bible, **I took my eyes off Jesus** and focused on people, seeking their approval. But it was God who I needed to trust all along. It was God who lifted me out of every storm, who protected me when no one else was there. **In my darkest days, during the loneliest nights, and through every uncertainty, God was always there.**

The next time you feel the urge to please someone, take a step back. Ask yourself, is it the approval of people or the approval of God that drives you? For me, it's God.

Remember: **Fake friends are like shadows, they're always near during your brightest moments but disappear in your darkest hour.**

Don't let the length of a friendship overshadow your growth. Surround yourself with those who inspire and uplift you, who push you to reach your full potential. True strength comes from standing firm in who you are and seeking the approval of the One who will never leave your side.

Stop watering dead plants. You don't owe anyone an explanation for choosing peace over performance. God didn't create you to be liked: He created you to be faithful. So stop chasing applause and start walking in alignment. Your worth isn't tied to who claps when you win, but who called you before the world even knew your name. That's God, and He's the only approval you need.

"The Lord is on my side; I will not fear. What can man do to me?" (Psalm 118:6)

Pray with me

Lord,

Set me free from the trap of people-pleasing. Remind me that I was made in Your image, not theirs. Help me release the need for validation from those who were never meant to understand my calling. Strengthen me to stand in truth, even when it costs me relationships. Let my heart beat for Your approval alone. Thank You for being my constant: my safe place.

In Jesus' name,
Amen.

Day 81

It's Going to Rain

A number of years ago, I was out riding my motorcycle on a beautiful summer day. The sky was clear, the air was warm, and everything just felt right. I was cruising around town, not a care in the world. But then, out of nowhere, the sky turned dark. Thunder boomed. Lightning flashed across the sky like fireworks on the Fourth of July. Then came the first drop of rain, slamming against my helmet hard enough to make me sit up straighter. Before I knew it, I was drenched.

As cars passed me by, I remember wondering, **What do they think of me out here getting soaked?** They were dry, safe, speeding ahead, while I was out there feeling exposed and unprepared. And honestly, I probably should've checked the weather before heading out! But hey, it was too late now. All I could do was keep going… and pray the whole way home.

Have you ever had a moment like that? When everything's fine one minute, and then, suddenly, the storm hits? Life's storms don't usually come with warning signs. One moment, you're on top of the world. The next, you're knocked down by something you never saw coming: a health scare, financial trouble, the loss of someone you love, or a season where God feels quiet and distant.

But here's the truth I want you to hold onto: **God is with you in every season. Always.**

Think about Noah for a minute. He spent **decades** building an ark: something no one had ever seen or done before. People probably laughed at him. They were partying, living life, not a cloud in the sky… and there he was: hammering away on a giant boat in the middle of dry land.

But Noah trusted God's word more than what he saw around him.

"Noah did everything just as God commanded him." (Genesis 6:22)

Still, imagine the **years** of waiting. The questions. The whispers. The doubt. He didn't have thunder in the forecast: **he had only God's voice.** No proof. No blueprint except obedience. **But he kept showing up. He kept building. That's faith.**

Why am I telling you this? Because sometimes God calls us to do things that don't make sense to anyone else. They may laugh. They may think we're crazy. **But your faith has to be louder than their opinions.** Obedience to God means saying yes even when the outcome isn't clear.

Maybe God is calling you to build something right now. Maybe it's healing from a past wound. Starting something new. Letting go of something familiar. Or maybe it's simply drawing closer to Him. Don't despise these quiet seasons; they're where your faith grow deeper.

And remember this: **Your storm may have surprised you, but it didn't surprise God.** Your struggles don't cancel His promises.

"When you pass through the waters, I will be with you." **(Isaiah 43:2)**

God is calling you to trust Him in the storm; whether it's already raging or just on the horizon. **Don't wait for perfect conditions or clearer signs. Start building your faith now. Step by step. Nail by nail. Just like Noah did.**

Listen for His voice above the noise. Obey even when it feels risky. **You don't have to have it all figured out: you just have to be faithful with what He's given you.**

So today, ask yourself: **What is God asking me to build or prepare for? What part of my faith needs to grow?**

Don't be afraid to take that first step. Remember, He is with you through every wave, every storm, and every quiet moment.

Your journey with God isn't about avoiding the storm. It's about walking through it with the One who holds you steady.

Don't wait for the sky to clear: **move when God speaks.** Build when it doesn't make sense. **Trust Him when the clouds gather and when the world questions your obedience.** Just like Noah, your faith isn't about forecasts, it's about following the voice of the One who sees the end from the beginning. So pick up your hammer, fix your eyes on Jesus, and keep going. **The rain may be coming, but so is the promise.**

Pray with me

Lord,

For everyone walking through a storm right now, I pray You meet them with strength and peace. Remind them You are right there in the boat with them. Help them trust You, prepare, and move forward: step by step, with confidence and faith. Thank You that no storm is stronger than Your promise.

In Jesus' name,
Amen.

Day 82

When God Rescued Me

Today, I want to share one of the most vulnerable stories of my life. It's not easy to open up like this, but I know someone reading this needs to hear it. God has placed it on my heart to share, and out of obedience to Him, I will.

No matter how life looks right now, you are not a mistake. Your existence is not an accident. You were created on purpose, for a purpose, by a God who sees the fullness of your worth, even when life tries to tell you otherwise. *"For I know the plans I have for you," declares the Lord, "plans to prosper you and not to harm you, plans to give you a hope and a future"* (**Jeremiah 29:11**).

Some of you have been on a roller coaster of pain and uncertainty, facing challenges you never thought you'd endure. You might feel like life has beaten you down and wonder if the breakthrough you're praying for will ever come. Let me assure you: your life has meaning. You are not forgotten, and God has a plan for you. *"The Lord is close to the brokenhearted and saves those who are crushed in spirit"* (**Psalm 34:18**).

In **Matthew 6:25-33**, Jesus reminds us not to worry about what we'll eat, drink, or wear because God knows exactly what we need. He hasn't forgotten about you. Even in the middle of your pain, He's asking you to seek Him and trust that He's already working on your behalf.

Here's the part of my story that's difficult to share, but it's also the part where God's glory shines the brightest.

There was a time in my life when I was homeless. Yes, homeless. College-educated, healthy, with so much potential, yet I found myself in one of the darkest seasons of my life.

How could this happen? It wasn't because of addiction or anything like that: it was because I made some bad financial decisions that spiraled out of control. Before I knew it, I was left with nowhere to go. *"For the Lord gives wisdom; from His mouth come knowledge and understanding"* (**Proverbs 2:6**). I needed wisdom, and God was about to show me that no situation is too far gone for His redemption.

Out of shame, I didn't tell my family. I didn't want them to see me as a failure. Instead, I confided in just one close friend, who graciously let me stay in his small studio apartment. He worked long hours, so I would spend the day wandering, praying desperately for God to help me. At night, I slept on the floor of his tiny space, feeling broken, lost, and ashamed.

But even then, God was with me.

One day, I reached a breaking point. I swallowed my pride and asked my friend if I could use his phone to call my sister. **That call changed everything.** When I told my sister the truth, she didn't shame me or judge me. She simply said, **"Come home."**

Those words were a lifeline: a reminder that I wasn't alone, that God hadn't abandoned me. Through my sister and my mother, God showed me His love and provision. They took me in, loved me, and helped me rebuild. *"I will never leave you nor forsake you"* (**Deuteronomy 31:8**).

Day by day, I grew stronger. God opened doors that I couldn't have opened on my own. He restored me, piece by piece, and showed me that He had never left my side; not even in my darkest moments.

When I share this story with others, many don't believe it. They see where I am now and can't imagine where I came from. But that's the power of God's grace. He takes our brokenness and turns it into a testimony of His goodness. *"For we are God's workmanship, created in Christ Jesus to do good works, which God prepared in advance for us to do"* (**Ephesians 2:10**).

The same God who rescued me wants to do the same for you. He's a loving Father who never abandons His children. **When I hit rock bottom, He became my foundation. When I was lost, He found me.**

God doesn't see you as a failure. He sees you as His child, uniquely crafted with a purpose that only you can fulfill. If you're feeling abandoned, ashamed, or uncertain about your future, let me remind you: God is with you. **He hasn't left, and He never will.**

Your current situation is not your final destination. God is doing something new, even if you can't see it yet. *"See, I am doing a new thing! Now it springs up; do you not perceive it? I am making a way in the wilderness and streams in the wasteland"* (**Isaiah 43:19**). Trust that God is working, even when it doesn't feel like it.

When I look back on that season, I realize that God never stopped loving me. He wasn't waiting to condemn me for my mistakes; He was waiting to welcome me home. Jesus knows what it's like to be rejected, misunderstood, and without a place to lay His head. Yet He stayed faithful to His mission, enduring unimaginable pain so that we could be reconciled to the Father. When I finally surrendered my life to God, He didn't just fix my circumstances, He transformed my heart. He gave me a new perspective, a renewed purpose, and the courage to share my story so that others might find hope in Him.

If you're struggling, feeling like life has beaten you down, know that you don't have to face this alone. God is waiting for your yes. He's ready to take your pain, your mistakes, and your doubts and turn them into a story of redemption. "***The Lord is near to all who call on Him, to all who call on Him in truth***" **(Psalm 145:18)**.

Pray with me

Lord,

Thank You for loving me even when I feel unworthy. Thank You for never leaving me, even in my darkest moments. Today, I surrender my life to You. I give You my pain, my fears, and my future. Lord, lead me back to You and help me trust that You are working all things for my good. I choose You, God, and I ask You to guide me every step of the way.

In Jesus' name,
Amen.

Day 83

A Wake-Up Call for Your Purpose

Before you read another word: **stop**.

Wherever you are, whatever you're doing, take a breath. Lift your heart. Whisper a thank you. Raise your hands, if you can. This is holy ground, and God is near. He holds your very breath in His hands. Don't rush past this moment. Honor Him. He is worthy of more than words can say.

Now listen closely: not just with your ears, but with your heart.

Every choice you make, or avoid is shaping your future. Every step is leading you somewhere: either closer to your purpose or further from it. That's not just poetic. it's truth. Real, eternal, weighty truth. Your life is not random. Heaven is paying attention.

We live in a world that's obsessed with imitation. We chase after dreams that were never ours to begin with. We wear masks just to be accepted by people we were never meant to follow. We hunger for relevance and applause more than we hunger for righteousness. But if the approval of others becomes your guide, you'll keep wandering, always busy, never fulfilled. God says otherwise:

"This day I call the heavens and the earth as witnesses... I have set before you life and death, blessings and curses. Now choose life..." **(Deuteronomy 30:19)**

You weren't created to copy someone else. You were designed by God: crafted with purpose, with destiny written into your DNA. Before you were even born, He saw you. He dreamed over you. He planted divine potential in you.

"For we are God's masterpiece. He has created us anew in Christ Jesus, so we can do the good things He planned for us long ago." **(Ephesians 2:10)**

But here's the problem: too many of us are still waiting. Waiting for someone to say we're ready. Waiting for perfect conditions. Waiting for a green light, a clear sign, a loud "Go."
But when God says move, hesitation becomes disobedience.

"If you are willing and obedient, you will eat the good things of the land." **(Isaiah 1:19)**

Yes, it's scary. Obedience will stretch you. Surrender might cost you. But staying stuck will cost you even more.

You weren't chosen to impress people. You were anointed to glorify a King. Some people will misunderstand your calling, and that's okay. They were never meant to interpret what God placed inside of you. Keep your eyes on Him.

Something has shifted in this season. Can you feel it?

Heaven is calling. God is drawing you closer, not to a platform or performance, but to Him. He's not impressed by our busy schedules. He doesn't want your leftovers. He wants your heart.

"Trust in the Lord with all your heart and lean not on your own understanding; in all your ways acknowledge Him, and He will make your paths straight." (Proverbs 3:5–6)

I know what it's like to look the part, say the right things, do all the right **"Christian"** things, and still feel numb. I was surviving, not living. Until one quiet moment: simple, sacred; God arrested my heart. Like Saul on the road to Damascus, He interrupted everything to awaken something deeper.

And now I know: He never wanted my perfection. He wanted my trust. My time. My yes.

He wants yours too.

God sees you: tired, unsure, hiding behind fear. But He also sees what you can become when your life is fully surrendered to Him. He sees strength in you. He sees purpose. He sees beauty rising from the ashes.

This is your moment. Your wake-up call.

No more shrinking back. No more waiting for **"someday."** No more doubting your place in God's story.

You've been **chosen**. You've been **called**. You've been **equipped**.

"You did not choose me, but I chose you and appointed you so that you might go and bear fruit—fruit that will last." (John 15:16)

Now is the time. Step forward: **not in your own strength, but in His**. Surrender your fear. Say yes to His voice. And watch what happens when you finally walk in the purpose you were made for.

Pray with me

Father God,

Thank You for speaking so clearly. Thank You for calling us, even when we feel unworthy or unsure. Today, we surrender. No more delay. No more fear. No more comparison. We lay down our excuses and pick up Your promise.

Give us courage to obey, clarity to follow, and strength to keep going when it gets hard. We want to walk in Your will, not ours. Help us to trust You completely, love You deeply, and honor You boldly.

We choose life. We choose truth. We choose You.

In Jesus' name,
Amen.

Day 84

The Gift of True Giving

Have you ever stopped to ask yourself why you give? Is it because you feel like you should, or because you're hoping for something in return? Maybe you've given to someone and secretly waited for a **"thank you,"** a favor back, or even praise that never came.

If we're honest, many of us have given with strings attached. But true giving? It's different. It's not a transaction. It's love in action, no conditions, no hidden motives.

The best example we have is God Himself. **John 3:16** says:

"For God so loved the world that He gave His one and only Son, that whoever believes in Him shall not perish but have eternal life."

God gave Jesus, not because He needed anything from us, but because He loves us so deeply. Jesus's life, death, and resurrection are the ultimate gifts: freely given so we could know forgiveness, hope, and new life.

This kind of giving: selfless, sacrificial, rooted in love, is what we're invited to live out.

Growing up, I watched my mother live this out daily. She didn't have much, but she gave everything she could: her time, energy, and love, to anyone in need. She never asked for anything back. She didn't do it for praise. She did it because that's who she was. At the time, I didn't understand how someone with so little could give so much. But her example stuck with me. Later, when I hit a low point and cried out to God for help, I made a promise:

"Lord, if You ever bless me, I will give freely, no strings attached."

And that promise wasn't just about money. It was about giving my time, attention, and heart; just as my mother did.

Giving isn't just about handing over cash. It's about seeing the needs around you and saying, **"God, I'm available."** It could be offering your time to someone who's lonely, sending a text of encouragement, or providing a meal for a family going through a hard time.

Sometimes, giving looks like using your skills to help a neighbor, mentoring someone who feels lost, or simply listening when someone needs to talk. Even your prayers are a gift, lifting others to God in faith.

And don't overlook forgiveness. Letting go of bitterness and extending grace is one of the most powerful gifts you can give: **to others and yourself.**

What matters most is not the size of the gift, but the love behind it.

2 Corinthians 9:7 reminds us: *"Each of you should give what you have decided in your heart to give, not reluctantly or under compulsion, for God loves a cheerful giver."*

God isn't looking for forced giving. He loves when we give because we want to, not because we have to. When we give with joy and open hands, we reflect His love to the world and honor Him in the process.

Take a moment and **ask yourself**:

- What has God given me that I can share with others?
- Where is He inviting me to give, even in small ways?
- Am I giving to be seen, or am I giving from love?

Every act of giving; whether big or small, has the power to **change someone's life**. God gave to us without hesitation, and now we get to do the same.

You don't need to have it all together to give. You don't need to wait until you have more. God can use what you have right now.

Look for opportunities **this week** to give freely, love deeply, and trust that God will take care of the rest. True giving isn't about recognition or reward. **It's about living out the love of Jesus, one small act at a time.**

Pray with me

Father God,

Thank You for all You've given me. Help me to give with a joyful, open heart, without expecting anything in return. Show me the needs around me and give me the courage to respond. Let my giving reflect Your love and bring You glory. In Jesus's name, Amen.

In Jesus' name,
Amen.

Day 85

Taking a Step Back

What if the pause you're resisting is the doorway to God's best for you?

I remember a time when my daughter was preparing for a *TED Talk* at her school. She struggled to find a topic that would connect with everyone but finally chose something simple yet powerful: **taking a step back**.

She spent hours practicing, and just days before the talk, she asked me to listen. As she spoke, her words hit me hard. She talked about how we all need to slow down, recharge, and focus on what truly matters. And she was right.

We live in a world that constantly pushes us to do more, be more, and chase after the next thing. It's easy to get caught up in the busyness, setting new goals and plans, hoping they'll bring us peace or fulfillment.

But here's a question we don't ask often enough: **"How can I grow closer to God in this season?"**

We often come to God with lists of what we need or want. And while He cares deeply about our desires, God also wants something even greater: **a close, personal relationship with us**.

Think about it: Spending time with my daughter is one of my greatest joys. I can only imagine how God feels when His children slow down and spend time with Him, **not just to ask for things but simply to be with Him**.

Recently, I was working on a project and hit a wall. I was frustrated, stuck, and trying to figure it out on my own. Then it hit me: I hadn't invited God into the process.

So, I stopped. I prayed, asking for His help and forgiveness for trying to do it alone. Almost immediately, the ideas started flowing again. It was as if God whispered, **"You don't have to do this by yourself. I'm here. Let Me help."**

That moment reminded me that God cares about every detail of our lives; big and small. He wants to walk with us through our dreams, struggles, and even the ordinary moments we overlook.

The Bible says, *"For where your treasure is, there your heart will be also."* (Matthew 6:21)

It challenges me to reflect on what I'm prioritizing. Are we chasing things that won't last: like success, money, or approval, **while neglecting the One who holds our future?**

Another verse asks, *"What good is it for someone to gain the whole world, yet forfeit their soul?"* (Mark 8:36)

It's a reminder that even good things can distract us from what matters most: our relationship with God.

Taking a step back isn't just about slowing down; it's about intentionally inviting God into every part of our lives. **When we pause, we begin to see His hand in everything.** We remember that He's the giver of every good thing and the One who sustains us in every season.

So right now, take a deep breath. Pause. Thank God for His faithfulness, even in the challenges that have helped you grow. Give Him your worries, your plans, and your dreams.

When we put God first, everything else finds its rightful place.

Don't wait for a perfect moment to draw near to Him. **The perfect moment is now.**

Take that step today. Carve out time, even if it's just a few minutes, to pray, reflect, or read His Word. Let God be part of your everyday life: your highs, your lows, your decisions, and your dreams.

When you do, you will see Him move in ways you never expected, and you will experience a peace and purpose that only He can give.

Pray with me

Lord,

Thank You for always being near, even when life feels overwhelming. Help me to slow down and make space for You in my day. Teach me to put You first in all I do and to trust that You care about every part of my life. Forgive me for the times I've tried to do it all on my own. I invite You into my plans, my dreams, and my struggles. Help me to see Your hand in every moment and to find rest in Your presence. I choose to take a step back and put You at the center of my life. Thank You for Your love and faithfulness.

In Jesus' name,
Amen.

Day 86

God Doesn't Wait for Your Permission

What do you do when God changes the plans you were so sure about?

You planned for it. Prayed over it. Maybe even started building it. Then out of nowhere, you feel a quiet nudge in your spirit or a hard stop you never saw coming. And you're left asking, **"God… what are You doing?"**

Believe me, I know that feeling.

I was deep into the final edits for the sequel I thought was my next assignment. It made sense. It fit the plan, and I was months away from publishing when God interrupted. Suddenly, He rerouted me to write about spiritual warfare. Then, He led me somewhere else I hadn't planned. Neither was on my radar, but both were on His. And here's what I learned:

God will interrupt your good plans to insert His greater purpose.

Shifts don't always come easy. Sometimes God whispers; sometimes, He shakes things up. But when God moves you, it's never to leave you empty: it's to place you exactly where you need to be.

Alignment isn't always comfortable. I've experienced it beyond writing. Moving from Boston to Virginia was never in my plan. It was a big shift, and at the time, I didn't understand it. But God saw what I couldn't. He was moving me to find Him in ways I couldn't have there. Looking back, I see His plan was better, even when it didn't make sense at first.

Imagine spending years earning a degree, building a career around it, only for God to lead you in a different direction. You might wonder why the sudden change or why you weren't warned.

It doesn't erase your past, it repurposes it. That degree, job, those skills? God can use them in ways you never imagined. But you might not see it right away. That's where faith steps in. Don't run like Jonah, who almost brought disaster because he didn't want to follow God's call. But once God had his attention, Jonah's obedience saved many. You can be on a good path, chasing good goals, but if it's not God's plan for this season, He will nudge or push you toward something greater. Don't resist: trust and believe

"We can make our plans, but the Lord determines our steps."
(Proverbs 16:9)

I had to let go of what made sense to take up what I hadn't prepared for. That's when peace came. Not because I understood everything, but because I trusted the One who does.

It's not easy, but it's necessary. Maybe you've been in a job for years, established in careers, or tied to places and people that feel safe, and then God shifts you. It's not to bring failure but to lead you into His promise.

"For I know the plans I have for you," says the Lord, "plans to prosper you and not to harm you, plans to give you hope and a future." (Jeremiah 29:11)

Abram in Genesis 12 was settled, wealthy, and comfortable. Then God told him to leave everything familiar and step into the unknown. That shift birthed a nation.

Amos in Amos 7 wasn't a prophet or trained for ministry, but God called him to speak to a nation in crisis.

Esther in Esther 4 lived in safety until God called her to risk everything to save others.

These shifts weren't easy. They were necessary. And they weren't just about them, they were about generations to come. God doesn't always call the qualified: He qualifies the called. Your occupation isn't a limit; it might be your launching pad.

Take a moment and ask:

- Where is God calling me to walk that I've been afraid to go?

- What key has He placed in my hand that I've been hesitant to use?

God is still shifting lives. Sometimes gently, sometimes suddenly. But it's always for one reason: **His purpose.**

If you feel tension, uncertainty, or see an unexpected door opening, pause and ask: **"Lord, is this You shifting me?"**

Stay willing and watchful. Like Abraham, Amos, and Esther, you may be on the edge of something greater than you ever imagined.

Remember, not every shift is from God. But when God shifts you, and you choose trust over fear and surrender over control, you give Him all the glory and step into the future He's prepared for you.

Pause and ask: **"Lord, is this shift from You?"** If it is, move with bold faith, not fear. Surrender your plans so His purpose can unfold. Share what God is doing, and let your obedience become someone else's encouragement. This is your moment to walk in what He has prepared, giving Him all the glory as you step into your next chapter with Him leading the way.

Pray with me

Lord,

Lord, thank You for loving us enough to shift us when we settle for less than Your best. Give us courage to walk where You call us, even when it's uncomfortable. Help us to trust You when we don't see the full picture, knowing Your plans are good. Align our steps with Your purpose, and let our obedience bring You glory.

In Jesus' name,
Amen.

Day 87

Every Second Counts

I was having a conversation with my daughter the other day, and I asked her, **"What are you passionate about?"** She looked at me, smiled, and said, **"Dad, let's just go get lunch."** I smiled back, knowing she wasn't ready for one of my deep questions: lunch was all she had in mind. I get it. But I didn't let it go. I gave it a few more minutes, then had to jump into a meeting and promised myself I'd revisit the question later.

By the time the meeting ended, I started thinking about dinner plans, what I had to do after work, and so many other things. Before I knew it, the day was almost gone. I asked myself, **"Where did the time go?"**

That's when it hit me.

God gives us **24 hours** every day. That's **1,440 minutes**, or **86,400 seconds**. Each one is precious, and once it's gone, we can't get it back. We often say every penny counts, **but every second counts even more, because every second comes from the Creator of everything.**

Psalm 90:12 says, ***"Teach us to number our days, that we may gain a heart of wisdom."*** God wants us to use our time wisely and not waste a single moment.

We might think there's plenty of time, but the truth is, we don't have time to stay stuck or wait until we **"feel ready."** That's not how God's purpose moves in our lives.

When God calls you to something, He's not waiting for the perfect time. He's asking you to use the moment you have right now **(Ecclesiastes 11:4)**. Sometimes it feels like we have forever to figure it out, but waiting for the **"right moment"** can keep us frozen in place.

His Word is alive, and so is the gift He placed inside you. Heaven is waiting on your yes. You don't need all the answers: just the faith to take the step He's calling you to take.

Think about someone with a voice that could heal hearts or a gift that could bring hope. But fear keeps them silent, hiding what God placed inside them. That silence doesn't just hold them back; it holds back the light God meant to break through darkness. When we bury what God has given us, we're not just delaying our purpose, we're delaying someone else's breakthrough.

Jesus shared a story about three servants given talents. Two used what they were given, and their gifts grew. **But one, afraid to fail, buried his talent, and there were consequences.** Are you letting fear or busyness bury what God gave you? You've prayed for wisdom and breakthrough, which is good, but **James 2:17** tells us, ***"Faith by itself, if it is not accompanied by action, is dead."***

Sometimes we say we're waiting on God, **but the truth is, God is often waiting on us** to take the next step. **Waiting without moving can become disobedience dressed up as caution.** Don't let fear, perfectionism, or busyness keep you from stepping into what God has already equipped you to do.

Remember Moses? God called him to lead His people, but Moses doubted he was enough. He made excuses and delayed obeying because he didn't fully trust God's plan for him. Yet, when Moses finally stepped out in faith, God showed up in mighty ways. **Your story can be like Moses's too, once you trust and obey, God will do the rest.**

You might feel too busy or think you don't have enough time but you do. **It's not about more hours; it's about how you use the ones you have. When something truly matters, you make time for it.** Maybe you're not too busy, you're just missing the right priorities: your growth, your purpose, your rest, and your connection with God.

I've been there. I work, give to others, write, and follow God's call even when I'm tired or feel unqualified, **because obedience is far more powerful than perfection.**

If you're stuck, look in the mirror. The answer isn't your job, your schedule, or your past. It's you. And that's good news because with God's help, you can change.

So, what now? Will you keep saying, **"I'll start tomorrow,"** and bury what God placed in you? Or will you stop, pray, surrender, and take a step, even a small one? **Ask God to reveal your gift, teach you to use it, and breathe new life into it.** He will, **but He won't force you. The choice is yours.** Don't wait. Every moment counts.

Pray with me

Lord,

Father, thank You for every breath and every second You've given me. Forgive me for the times I've wasted time, hidden my gifts, and believed lies about who I am. Show me what You've placed inside me and teach me how to use it. Help me to move past fear, give me strength to start again, and courage to keep going. I want to walk fully in what You've called me to do, not tomorrow, but today.

In Jesus' name,
Amen.

Day 88

No More Noise. The Cymbal has Sounded.
It's Time to Walk.

I had a dream recently, and the words I heard have been resting heavily on my heart and mind. I believe they aren't just for me, but for you, too.

"There is no more noise. The cymbal has sounded. It is time to walk."

It wasn't loud. It wasn't whispered. It was clear. It was final. I woke up with a **peace that felt holy**: the kind that comes when God speaks, and everything else falls away.

Sometimes we wait for the perfect sign before we move. We think we need another confirmation, another open door, another reason to believe we're ready. **But what if God has already made it clear? What if the writing is already on the wall, and we're just afraid to take the first step?**

I've been guilty of ignoring or running from God's voice more times than I'd like to admit. **Staying at tables God told me to leave. Taking a right when I should have taken a left. Choosing chaos over peace. Listening to the wrong voices**

when the writing on the wall was clear and the elephant in the room was impossible to ignore. Like Gideon, asking God for sign after sign (**Judges 6**) when the real issue wasn't God's faithfulness, but my fear to trust what He had already said. We've all done it, clinging to what feels safe, not realizing that doing things our way keeps us trapped in a prison of confusion when freedom is within reach if we would just walk in faith.

The dream I had spoke to me. **It gave me clarity I could no longer ignore.** Now that I know what I know, there's no turning back. God's voice and commands should never be silenced by our fear or lack of faith. And now that I have the key to freedom, I can't put it away anymore. **People are waiting on us to walk in what God has called us to do.**

In Scripture, God often uses sound to mark the moment when waiting ends and movement begins. The trumpet blast that told Israel it was time to break camp. The shout that brought down the walls of Jericho. The rushing wind that filled the room where the disciples were waiting, marking the coming of the Holy Spirit and the start of something entirely new. **None of those sounds were noise. They were signals.**

When God signals, there is no room for hesitation.

I think about Abraham leaving everything familiar because God said, **"Go."** I think about Peter stepping out of the boat because Jesus said, **"Come."** I think about the Israelites leaving Egypt because God said, **"It's time."** They didn't have the full picture, but **they had the signal. And the signal was enough**.

I don't know where you are in your journey, but maybe you've been circling the same decision, telling yourself you'll wait until you feel more secure. Maybe you've sensed God nudging you to forgive someone, to step into something new, to leave behind what's comfortable, to start what He's placed in your heart, but you're waiting for fear to quiet down before you move. **But what if fear won't quiet until you take the step?**

Romans 10:17 says, *"Faith comes by hearing, and hearing by the word of God."* We love the hearing part, but faith is proven when we walk on what we've heard.

Sometimes we overcomplicate obedience, waiting for everything to make sense before we move. But when God speaks, clarity often comes **after** we walk, **not before**.

The noise that keeps us frozen: overthinking, fear, **the opinions of others** doesn't have the final word. **When God signals, it silences the noise, and what remains is a simple, holy call to move.**

I believe this is that moment for many of us.

It's time to forgive. It's time to leave behind the safety of the boat. It's time to step into the unknown with Him. It's time to launch what He has placed in your spirit. It's time to believe that God is with you in what He has called you to do.

It's not about your readiness. It's about His faithfulness. **The cymbal has sounded. The waiting is over. It's time to walk.**

If you sense this word is for you, take a moment right now. Pause. Let the noise fall away. Breathe in the quiet. And take the first step you know God is asking you to take. You don't have to know every step. Just the next one. **The cymbal has sounded.**

Now, it's your turn to walk.

Pray with me

Lord,

Thank You for speaking clearly, for silencing the noise, and for calling us into Your timing. We surrender hesitation and fear, and we choose to walk with You. We trust that as we move, You will guide, provide, and lead us into what You have prepared. Let our steps bring You glory, and let our lives reflect the faith we have in You alone.

In Jesus' name,
Amen.

Day 89

Praying for Your Enemies

What's the first thing that comes to mind when you think about someone who's hurt you deeply?

Maybe it's a pain you can't imagine forgiving, or worse, someone who harmed someone you love.

For me, that person is the man who took my brother's life.

It was October 2020 when my world shattered. I'll never forget the call from my sister; her voice trembling as she told me something that didn't seem real: **my brother had been murdered**. Shot multiple times. At first, I thought it had to be a mistake, a horrible misunderstanding. But when another family member confirmed the news, the nightmare became real.

Seeing my brother lying in that casket, something inside me broke. I realized I would never hear his laugh again, never get another message from him, never share another moment. The finality of it crushed me. And then came the regret: for every call I didn't make, every visit I postponed, every chance I missed to say, **"I love you."**

That's when the anger took over. I didn't just want justice: I wanted revenge. I wanted the man who stole my brother to suffer, to feel the same pain he caused us. I kept thinking about the words, **"an eye for an eye."** But God's Word whispered something different:

"Love your enemies and pray for those who persecute you." (**Matthew 5:44**)

That verse wrecked me. How do you love someone who destroyed your family? How do you pray for someone you'd rather never think about again?

The truth is: I'm still learning.

I haven't arrived yet. I'm still grieving. Still healing. Still angry sometimes. I miss my brother. I read our last text messages often, clinging to his words, wishing I could send just one more. Some days, the heavyness of the loss feels unbearable. Could I have done more? What were his last thoughts? So many things ran through my mind, but one thing was certain. He was gone.

But in this process, I've learned something about God's heart. **He never asks us to ignore our pain: He invites us to bring it to Him.**

"The Lord is close to the brokenhearted and saves those who are crushed in spirit." (**Psalm 34:18**)

Forgiveness isn't forgetting. It isn't excusing what was done. It's releasing the burden; slowly, painfully, into the hands of a God who understands betrayal and injustice better than anyone.

"Do not take revenge, but leave room for God's wrath, for it is written: 'It is mine to avenge; I will repay,' says the Lord." **(Romans 12:19)**

God is patient with us. He walks with us in the long journey toward forgiveness. He doesn't demand we move faster than our hearts can bear. He simply asks us to take one step at a time, toward Him.

"Be kind and compassionate to one another, forgiving each other, just as in Christ God forgave you." **(Ephesians 4:32)**

I'm still learning to forgive. I haven't let go of all the hurt, but I'm giving God permission to start untangling it.

Maybe you're in that place too: somewhere between grief and grace, between pain and peace. And if you are, I want you to know: **God is not rushing you. He's sitting with you in the heartbreak. He sees every tear, every memory, every wave of sorrow. And He's not going anywhere.**

Pray with me

Lord,

You see every wound that hasn't healed. You know the depth of my anger, the ache of my loss, and the burden of what was taken. Help me begin, even if it's just a whisper, to move toward forgiveness. Not because it's easy, but because I don't want this pain to define me. Teach me to release it to You. Heal the parts of my heart that still feel broken. Give me grace for myself as I heal, and strength to trust You with what I can't fix.

In Jesus' name,
Amen.

Day 90

Who Told You That You Were Naked?

Have you ever opened your Bible, and it felt like God was speaking right to you? Like He was reaching into that quiet moment, uncovering something you didn't even know you were searching for?

That's what happened to me after a long week. I was tired and searching for something to lift me, something to remind me who I am and why I'm here. I opened to Genesis 3, a chapter I've read many times before, but this time, one verse stopped me.

"Who told you that you were naked?" (Genesis 3:11)

It's one of the most powerful questions God has ever asked.

God wasn't just talking about Adam's body. He was talking about **how Adam saw himself after sin entered the world**. Before that, Adam and Eve were naked and unashamed. They walked in full freedom: fully known and fully loved by God. But the moment they listened to another voice, everything changed. Shame crept in. Fear took hold. Hiding became their instinct. Their identity shifted, not because God changed, but because they believed a lie.

The truth is, **God never told Adam he was naked. Shame did. Fear did. Lies did.** And those same lies still whisper to us today, trying to tell us who we are, and who we are not.

Now let me ask you: Who told you you weren't enough? Who told you that you have no purpose? Who told you that you were too broken to be loved? Who told you your past defines your future? **Because God never said that about you.**

When did you start feeling naked? Maybe you don't call it **"naked,"** but you know the feeling: The fear that you'll never measure up. The voice that says you're behind everyone else. The guilt that whispers you've messed up too much to be used by God.

I've felt that too. There were seasons when I couldn't look in the mirror without picking myself apart. I tried to cover it up with busyness, people-pleasing, and pretending everything was fine. But those are just modern fig leaves.

Like Adam and Eve, **we sew coverings to hide what we're ashamed of.** We think we have to perform, people-please, or perfect our way into being loved and seen.

But here's the beautiful part: **God didn't leave Adam and Eve covered in fig leaves. He made coverings for them Himself. He covered them through a sacrifice, pointing us to Jesus, who would one day cover us completely with His righteousness.**

If you're tired of living under lies that don't belong to you, **let's break that agreement right now**. It doesn't have to be complicated. It just needs to be real.

Take a moment, breathe, and **say this out loud**:

God, I break agreement with every lie that says I'm not enough, not loved, or not worthy. I reject shame, fear, and comparison. I receive Your truth that I am loved, covered, and chosen. I am not naked; I am clothed in Christ. Help me to see myself the way You see me. In Jesus' name, Amen.

So today, and every day after, I charge you to keep walking toward God's voice. You don't have to have it all together to come to Him. God isn't looking for your perfection; He's looking for your heart.

If you're still struggling, that's okay. Healing is a journey, not a race. What matters is that you keep coming back to His voice: the voice that calls you **"Beloved," "Mine," and "Chosen."** The voice that says: "Who told you that? Because I never said that about you."

Take a moment today to pause and let God search your heart. Write down:

- What lie have I believed about myself?
- Who or what planted that lie?
- What does God say about me instead?

Let the Holy Spirit meet you in that quiet place and replace every lie with truth.

Hear me clearly: You are not too far gone. You are not behind. You are not forgotten. You are not naked. You are covered, loved, and chosen. **You are His.**

Pray with me

Father God,

I come to You, ready to let go of the lies I've believed about myself. I lay down shame, fear, and every word spoken over me that doesn't match what You say. I choose to receive Your truth that I am loved, chosen, and covered by Jesus. Break every stronghold in my mind that keeps me stuck, and replace it with Your freedom and peace. Teach me to see myself through Your eyes, and give me the courage to walk in the purpose You have for me. Thank You for Your love that never fails. I receive it now, in Jesus' name, Amen.

In Jesus' name,
Amen.

www.ingramcontent.com/pod-product-compliance
Lightning Source LLC
Chambersburg PA
CBHW050441150626
46551CB00028B/788